S. Hrg. 112–228

IMPLEMENTATION OF THE NEW STRATEGIC ARMS REDUCTION TREATY (START) AND PLANS FOR FUTURE REDUCTIONS IN NUCLEAR WARHEADS AND DELIVERY SYSTEMS POST-NEW START TREATY

HEARING

BEFORE THE

SUBCOMMITTEE ON STRATEGIC FORCES

OF THE

COMMITTEE ON ARMED SERVICES
UNITED STATES SENATE

ONE HUNDRED TWELFTH CONGRESS

FIRST SESSION

MAY 4, 2011

Printed for the use of the Committee on Armed Services

Available via the World Wide Web: http://www.fdsys.gov/

U.S. GOVERNMENT PRINTING OFFICE

72–462 PDF   WASHINGTON : 2012

For sale by the Superintendent of Documents, U.S. Government Printing Office
Internet: bookstore.gpo.gov   Phone: toll free (866) 512–1800; DC area (202) 512–1800
Fax: (202) 512–2104   Mail: Stop IDCC, Washington, DC 20402–0001

COMMITTEE ON ARMED SERVICES

CARL LEVIN, Michigan, *Chairman*

JOSEPH I. LIEBERMAN, Connecticut
JACK REED, Rhode Island
DANIEL K. AKAKA, Hawaii
E. BENJAMIN NELSON, Nebraska
JIM WEBB, Virginia
CLAIRE McCASKILL, Missouri
MARK UDALL, Colorado
KAY R. HAGAN, North Carolina
MARK BEGICH, Alaska
JOE MANCHIN III, West Virginia
JEANNE SHAHEEN, New Hampshire
KIRSTEN E. GILLIBRAND, New York
RICHARD BLUMENTHAL, Connecticut

JOHN McCAIN, Arizona
JAMES M. INHOFE, Oklahoma
JEFF SESSIONS, Alabama
SAXBY CHAMBLISS, Georgia
ROGER F. WICKER, Mississippi
SCOTT P. BROWN, Massachusetts
ROB PORTMAN, Ohio
KELLY AYOTTE, New Hampshire
SUSAN M. COLLINS, Maine
LINDSEY GRAHAM, South Carolina
JOHN CORNYN, Texas
DAVID VITTER, Louisiana

RICHARD D. DeBOBES, *Staff Director*
DAVID M. MORRISS, *Minority Staff Director*

————

SUBCOMMITTEE ON STRATEGIC FORCES

E. BENJAMIN NELSON, Nebraska, *Chairman*

JOSEPH I. LIEBERMAN, Connecticut
JACK REED, Rhode Island
MARK UDALL, Colorado
MARK BEGICH, Alaska
JEANNE SHAHEEN, New Hampshire
KIRSTEN E. GILLIBRAND, New York

JEFF SESSIONS, Alabama
JAMES M. INHOFE, Oklahoma
ROGER F. WICKER, Mississippi
ROB PORTMAN, Ohio
JOHN CORNYN, Texas
DAVID VITTER, Louisiana

(II)

CONTENTS

CHRONOLOGICAL LIST OF WITNESSES

IMPLEMENTATION OF THE NEW STRATEGIC ARMS REDUCTION TREATY (START) AND PLANS FOR FUTURE REDUCTIONS IN NUCLEAR WARHEADS AND DELIVERY SYSTEMS POST-NEW START TREATY

MAY 4, 2011

IMPLEMENTATION OF THE NEW STRATEGIC ARMS REDUCTION TREATY (START) AND PLANS FOR FUTURE REDUCTIONS IN NUCLEAR WARHEADS AND DELIVERY SYSTEMS POST-NEW START TREATY

WEDNESDAY, MAY 4, 2011

U.S. SENATE,
SUBCOMMITTEE ON STRATEGIC FORCES,
COMMITTEE ON ARMED SERVICES,
Washington, DC.

The subcommittee met, pursuant to notice, at 2:31 p.m. in room SR–232A, Russell Senate Office Building, Senator E. Benjamin Nelson (chairman of the subcommittee) presiding.

Committee members present: Senators Nelson, Udall, Shaheen, and Sessions.

Committee staff members present: Leah C. Brewer, nominations and hearings clerk; and Jennifer L. Stoker, security clerk.

Majority staff members present: Madelyn R. Creedon, counsel; and Richard W. Fieldhouse, professional staff member.

Minority staff member present: Daniel A. Lerner, professional staff member.

Staff assistants present: Hannah I. Lloyd and Breon N. Wells.

Committee members' assistants present: Ann Premer, assistant to Senator Ben Nelson; Casey Howard, assistant to Senator Udall; Chad Kreikemeier, assistant to Senator Shaheen; and Lenwood Landrum and Sandra Luff, assistants to Senator Sessions.

OPENING STATEMENT OF SENATOR E. BENJAMIN NELSON, CHAIRMAN

Senator NELSON. Good afternoon. The subcommittee meets this afternoon to discuss implementation of the New Strategic Arms Reduction Treaty (START) and the next steps for possible future reductions in strategic systems beyond those in the New START treaty. With us today we have: Principal Deputy Under Secretary of Defense for Policy, Dr. Jim Miller; Commander of U.S. Strategic Command (STRATCOM), General C. Robert Kehler; former Secretary of Defense, Dr. William Perry; and Dr. Keith Payne, Professor and Head, Graduate Department of Defense and Strategic Studies, Missouri State University at the Washington Campus.

Dr. Perry was the Chairman of the Perry-Schlesinger Strategic Posture Commission. Dr. Payne was a member of that Posture Commission. Other than General Kehler, all of our witnesses this afternoon have testified on previous occasions on the topic of strategic arms reduction during the Senate consideration of the New START treaty. The only reason General Kehler didn't is because he was appointed subsequent to that.

The organization of the hearing today is not the norm as we're having just one panel of witnesses, both government and private sector. Normally this hearing would have been conducted in two panels, but to allow us to take full advantage of Dr. Perry's limited availability today we're having one panel.

In that regard, I would note that Dr. Perry has to leave at 3:15 p.m. so he can catch his flight back to California for a speech. As a result, I'll forego additional opening remarks until later in the hearing, and I'd ask as well our witnesses to forego some opening remarks, but ask each witness to make closing remarks at the end of the hearing.

Dr. Perry, we would like to have any closing remarks from you as well prior to departure at 3:15 p.m. Several people are watching the clock so that time doesn't get away from us and we keep you on schedule.

All written statements that have been received will, of course, be included in the record.

Now I turn to my ranking member, my good friend, Senator Sessions.

STATEMENT OF SENATOR JEFF SESSIONS

Senator SESSIONS. Thank you, Mr. Chairman. It's a pleasure to work with you. I know your expertise and interest in these important matters.

Today's hearing is a continuation of our dialogue on U.S. strategic posture in a post-New START treaty environment in what appears to be the administration's intention to change U.S. nuclear doctrine and targeting guidance in an attempt to pursue further reductions in the nuclear stockpile on the path to what many of us feel is a misguided and dangerous idea of a world without nuclear weapons.

I wish it were so, but I believe that it's beyond unrealistic. It really could be dangerous if it clouds our thinking.

When we commissioned the bipartisan Perry-Schlesinger Strategic Posture Commission in 2008, we looked to a distinguished panel of 12 independent experts to address the current state and future role of nuclear weapons and strategic deterrence, among other crucial national security issues. Dr. Perry, thank you for your leadership. Dr. Payne, thank you for serving as a valuable member of that commission.

Among their many findings and recommendations, the Posture Commission emphasized the importance of achieving balance by sustaining a nuclear deterrence for the indefinite future while reducing reliance on nuclear weapons for deterrence. It is a balanced approach, and I'm concerned that the administration may be on the verge of abandoning that approach, opting instead for a nuclear weapons policy focused on unilateral reductions, an approach the Posture Commission warned would "weaken the deterrence of foes and the assurance of allies."

While the Posture Commission expressed differing visions of what might be possible in the long term, they urged extreme caution towards pursuing any approach characterized as being lopsided and concluded that: "So long as nuclear dangers remain, the United States must have a strong deterrence that is effective in meeting its security needs and those of its allies."

So I look forward to hearing from Dr. Perry and Dr. Payne as we go forward to discuss the balance that we need to achieve.

Recent statements by the President's National Security Advisor have prompted new questions in my mind about the administration's intent to pursue additional reductions. In his speech before the Carnegie Endowment, National Security Advisor, Tom Donilon, the President's right-hand man, stated that the administration is currently "making preparations for the next round of nuclear reductions" already, and that the Department of Defense (DOD) will be directed to "review our strategic requirements and develop options for further reductions in our current nuclear stockpile."

Mr. Donilon continued, stating that in meeting these objectives the White House will direct DOD to consider potential changes in targeting requirements and alert procedures. Furthermore, by inferring that the New START treaty signified a "shared goal of disarmament," his words, between the United States and Russia—so I question the reality and the seriousness of that goal, frankly.

The U.S. Senate did not consent to a goal of disarmament. That was not part of the New START treaty.

The U.S. Senate has also not agreed to or been consulted on unilateral nuclear reductions, which according to recent press reports the administration is also considering.

So I look forward to hearing our witnesses' assessments of Mr. Donilon's comments, to better understand from our DOD witnesses what actions they've been instructed to take, how such guidance could influence the ongoing modernization of the triad of nuclear delivery vehicles, and the potential operational impacts of such guidance on force posture, targeting, and alert procedures.

The outdated state of nuclear weapons complex and the overdue need for robust investment is an area of significant concern, and I think we share that. I commend the President for working with Congress to address it. In response to the Posture Commission's assessment and the urging of Congress, the administration has identified a need for more than $200 billion over the next 10 years to modernize and sustain our nuclear deterrence. This is a level of investment that appears to be absolutely necessary to create the kind of weapons systems we need. Maybe some efficiencies can occur, but fundamentally we need to meet the goal we set of modernizing our facilities and our weapons systems.

We should remember that during the Cold War we devoted about one-quarter of our defense budget to the nuclear deterrence mission. Today our current spending will account for only some 3 percent of the defense spending. With a sustained, whole-of-government commitment to modernizing our forces, we will be postured to better face the challenges of the future. The conditions for further reductions, in my opinion, however, do not exist today, and while a modernized and robust manufacturing and delivery capability will gradually instill greater confidence and increased deterrence, even then I remain unconvinced that the conditions will ever exist to facilitate reductions below the New START levels. I just think there's a danger in going below this level and I think we need to be careful and thoughtful about it. The future threat remains dynamic. We look forward to hearing your testimony.

Thank you, Mr. Chairman, and I welcome the witnesses.

Senator NELSON. Thank you, Senator Sessions.

Dr. Perry, I'll go with the first question here. You were the Chairman of the Strategic Posture Commission, as indicated, and one of the Posture Commission's findings was that reaching the ultimate goal of global nuclear elimination would require a fundamental change in the world geopolitical order.

Did the Posture Commission have a view on the conditions for future incremental reductions beyond those in the New START treaty, number one? Number two, in your view, what sort of changes, if any, in geopolitical order would merit additional reductions?

Dr. PERRY. The answer to the first question, Senator Nelson, is that the Commission did not look directly at the question of what should follow. It advocated support of the New START treaty, but did not seriously discuss the steps that would follow after that.

In my own view, what would be required there is very difficult, but worth doing, is coming to an agreement with the Russians on the tactical nuclear weapons, of which they have several thousand and of which we only have a few hundred. There's a real asymmetry in forces between the United States and Russia in that regard, and there's a real asymmetry in threat perception, which leads the Russians to believe they need those tactical nuclear weapons. They live in a different neighborhood than we live in.

I'm very much in favor of moving forward with a follow-on treaty. I think it's going to need to include tactical nuclear weapons. I think that will be a very difficult task, but not impossible to arrive at a way of dealing with that problem.

Senator NELSON. From your perspective, you don't see the administration moving unilaterally to reduce the arms?

Dr. PERRY. No, I do not. I think all of the actions that I've seen from the administration and all the statements that have been made suggest they're going to move hand-in-hand with the Russians, and I think it's possible that they will be able to find some mode of agreement with the Russians on a follow-on treaty. But it's a treaty which will be bilateral and I think will look forward. If there's any movement beyond that, it has to be beyond bilateral; it has to include other nations that have nuclear weapons.

Senator NELSON. On April 18 in the op-ed in the Financial Times that my colleague has mentioned, Tom Donilon, the President's National Security Advisor, discussed the need to begin the next round of nuclear weapons reductions as the New START treaty is implemented. He said that a review at President Obama's direction "will develop options for new reductions in the U.S. stockpile. Once complete, this will shape our approach to a new agreement with Russia."

Dr. Miller, has the review that Mr. Donilon mentioned started? Who is participating in that review and would there be a timeline for completion if there is such a review ongoing?

Dr. MILLER. Mr. Chairman, that review has not yet officially kicked off, but we've had some initial discussions about both its content and the timeline. We expect that when we do get presidential guidance to initiate the study it will take several months, and following that we would then expect to see changes to presidential guidance for nuclear weapons targeting, and all of this we expect to be consistent with the Nuclear Posture Review (NPR).

Following any changes in presidential guidance, we would expect to see changes to the Secretary's guidance, changes in the guidance from the Chairman, each of which, each layer from the President to the Secretary to the Chairman, is more detailed, and then the development of any revisions to operational plans by the Commander of STRATCOM.

Mr. Chairman, I want to emphasize that all of this activity is entirely consistent with what has happened in the past after the completion of NPRs and similar work, and that we are intending to undertake this consistent with the principles outlined in the NPR and intending to ensure that we continue to have effective deterrence and stability, that we have effective extended deterrence and assurance of our allies as well; and that, as Senator Sessions noted, the investments in our infrastructure and our delivery systems are critical as we move forward.

Senator NELSON. While the administration may be moving forward in anticipation of a new reduction, anything that it's doing is not intended to be unilateral; I heard Dr. Perry say something of that sort. Is that the way you see it?

Dr. MILLER. Senator Nelson, that's exactly correct. We said in the NPR that, while exact parity may not be as important as it was in the Cold War, there are still a number of good reasons why it's important that, if we go and as we go forward to any further reductions, that Russia join with us. That principle, articulated in the NPR, still remains valid and is a guiding principle for the analysis that we expect to undertake and implement in the NPR.

Senator NELSON. Thank you.

Senator Sessions, would you like to ask questions?

Senator SESSIONS. Yes. I'm looking at the Associated Press article of April 5 by Desmond Butler: "In the mean time," it says, "the administration is looking for other ways to cut its arsenal. A senior administration official, speaking on condition of anonymity because of the sensitivity of the issue, confirmed that the United States is considering these cuts independent of negotiations with Russia."

So do you know who made those comments and do they reflect the opinion of the administration, Dr. Miller?

Mr. MILLER. Senator, I don't know who made the comments and the policy of the administration has been and remains to move forward after—with any reductions beyond New START, in partnership with Russia, and to give priority to that. We have said in the past that we—and I believe that National Security Advisor Donilon made reference to this in his remark—that our intention is to propose reductions in strategic and non-strategic weapons, in both deployed and nondeployed weapons, in order to go after the asymmetry that Dr. Perry referred to, where Russia has much larger numbers of tactical nuclear weapons.

We could foresee some steps to improve transparency—we think that would be very helpful—to continue to work on strategic and tactical nuclear weapons, and ultimately to reduce their numbers.

Senator SESSIONS. I'll be frank with you. I appreciated the agreement that Congress asked for and insisted on as part of the START treaty negotiations to spend the $200 billion to modernize our arsenal and our facilities. But in the defense NPR the document had 31 references to the President's goal of zero nuclear weapons and a world without nuclear weapons. The President has repeatedly stated that he wants to lead by example.

In this article I just quoted from from AP, it quotes the President as promising: "To put an end to Cold War thinking, we will reduce the role of nuclear weapons in our national security strategy, and urge others to do the same." In other words, we will reduce and urge others to do the same.

Forgive me if it's making me feel like that this very strong commitment to zero nuclear weapons has put us in a position where we're going to lead without being assured that our nuclear competitors are participating equally.

Could you comment on that?

Dr. MILLER. Senator, thank you. Every President since the nuclear age began has advocated the eventual elimination of nuclear weapons with one exception. That was George W. Bush. Every President since Truman has advocated that as a goal. President Obama, I think, is therefore not unique in that goal, and he has noted explicitly that he does not expect it necessarily to occur in his lifetime.

Senator SESSIONS. Necessarily to occur, but it might. Do you think it's likely? Do you think it's likely we'll have zero nuclear weapons in President Obama's lifetime, recognizing he's even as a young man he is?

Dr. MILLER. Senator Sessions, I think it would take, as Dr. Perry referred to, fundamental changes in the security environment that are very difficult to foresee today.

Senator SESSIONS. You would agree that somebody that wrote the defense NPR took very seriously this goal, to a degree I've never seen before, to reduce nuclear weapons to zero.

I know Secretary Gates did the introductory letter and he made reference to zero nuclear weapons in his introduction. To what extent were you involved in that?

Dr. MILLER. I was very much involved in it, Senator.

Senator SESSIONS. Was it under your supervision?

Dr. MILLER. Sir, the NPR was under the supervision of the President. It was a report provided by Secretary Gates and I was honored to play a role in that.

Senator SESSIONS. What I would tell you is that according to Mr. Donilon, the National Security Advisor, the White House will direct DOD to consider "potential changes in targeting requirements and alert procedures."

If you want—the policy we have today, the numbers we've agreed on today match, do they not—General Cartwright I believe testified they did—the targeting and alert requirements this country has? Is that yes or no?

Dr. MILLER. The answer is yes, that the numbers agreed to under the New START are more than sufficient to meet the guidance that currently exists, which is the guidance that was inherited from the Bush administration.

Senator SESSIONS. I believe it was General Cartwright that said they meet the requirements. That's what's required to meet the targeting and alert requirements. If you want to reduce that number, then you need to get DOD to change the targeting requirements, do you not? Otherwise, your weapons system wouldn't meet your targeting requirements.

Dr. MILLER. Senator, we see it in the other direction, and that is that we're being asked to look at potential changes in nuclear targeting guidance and associated requirements and to then do so in a way that strengthens deterrence and extended deterrence and assurance of our allies, and also to do so in a way that over time will reduce the role of nuclear weapons.

Senator SESSIONS. The goal should be, am I not correct, to ensure the defense and security of the United States of America? That's your goal.

Dr. MILLER. Of course that's the goal, Senator.

Senator SESSIONS. If you're going to reduce the targeting requirement, I come back to the thing, it seems to me that the President's goal is permeating DOD. He's not asking DOD, what do you need to meet your targeting requirements? He's asking DOD, apparently through Mr. Donilon, to change the targeting requirements, therefore to meet his goal of reducing weapons.

Dr. MILLER. Senator, case number one in the analysis will be what we have today and the planned forces under New START, it will look at that with respect to current guidance. We already know that those two match up because that was the analysis done during the NPR relating to the New START treaty.

The analysis will then look at alternative approaches to targeting and to hedging and to other steps that are also intended—all of them are intended to meet our deterrence and assurance requirements. Then we'll look at the associated numbers there. That is intended to inform future presidential guidance.

The alternative would be to say the President should provide guidance which all previous Presidents have done without the benefit of that analysis. So my perspective is it's a good useful thing to have the President informed as to the possible consequences of different types of guidance. It doesn't mean that any one will necessarily be selected. That's the purpose of the analysis, to inform that and to do it in a way that will help understand the implications of each for deterrence, extended deterrence, and assurance in particular.

Senator SESSIONS. Will you assure us that the military professionals, I hope, that are engaged in this will be protected and allowed to produce their independent, best independent judgment of what kind of targeting procedures we need?

Dr. MILLER. Yes, sir. Explicitly, STRATCOM played a central role in the NPR, including our analysis of what was appropriate under New START, and that will be the case in this analysis as well. The same will be true of the Joint Staff—you mentioned General Cartwright—and the Services also and the Chiefs played a critical role in our analysis in NPR. That will be the case for this analysis as well.

Senator SESSIONS. I believe the state of the record today is that it was General Cartwright, if I'm not mistaken—General Chilton, excuse me. I was confused about that. General Chilton has testified this is the force structure we need. His quote is: "I think the arsenal we have is exactly what is needed today to provide the deterrent."

So all of a sudden, as soon as we sign the New START treaty, the President, who has repeatedly said his goal is to go to zero nuclear weapons, his goal is to set an example for the world, his staff person I'll acknowledge anonymously says that they might do it independent of Russian participation. It just causes me concern that there will be pressure on DOD to produce targeting policies to meet and justify the reduction. I've been around here long enough to know that can happen, and I'm uneasy about it.

My time is up. Thank you, Mr. Chairman.

Senator NELSON. Thank you, Senator Sessions.

Senator Udall.

Senator UDALL. Thank you, Mr. Chairman.

Welcome, gentlemen. I have some specific questions, but I did want to comment on the line of thinking that my friend from Alabama just explored. Dr. Miller, you said every President with the exception of George W. Bush starting with General Eisenhower has called for an ongoing reduction in nuclear arms consistent with the national security needs of the United States?

Dr. MILLER. Senator, every President starting with President Truman has called for the elimination of nuclear weapons, except for President George W. Bush.

Senator UDALL. Is it fair to say that you look at the arc of history over those 60-some years now, that the civilized world, the developed world, with two exceptions I can think of, Iran and North Korea—and some would argue particularly the latter country is far from being developed—have come to understand that the reduction in nuclear arms can actually result in a safer, more stable world, as opposed to an arms race without limits?

Dr. MILLER. Senator, I think that's generally correct. We've also seen over this same period of time a number of countries pursuing nuclear weapons principally because of their regional security conditions. You can think of, for example, Pakistan in that category.

Senator UDALL. That's fair enough.

Dr. MILLER. India as well.

Senator UDALL. Secretary Perry and Dr. Miller, I note that National Security, Advisor Donilon, wrote an op-ed in the Financial Times focused, I think, in particular on the reduction of tactical nukes in the European theater, as did Minister Ivanov and former Secretary of State Albright as well.

It seems to me that was a part of the debate we had on the floor of the Senate last year, that being can we do more to reduce tactical nukes, are we not putting ourselves at a disadvantage because of the Russian arsenal? So my interpretation of what they're doing is following through on the promises and the commitments that were made in the Senate and by our nuclear arms experts to continue to pursue ways to meet that concern.

Would you each care to comment?

Dr. PERRY. I think in my judgment an important goal of any follow-on treaty to New START would be to address the tactical nuclear weapons issues. This will be a very difficult issue to address because of the tremendous asymmetry between the United States and Russia in that case, the asymmetry being not only in the number of tactical nuclear weapons possessed—we have a few hundred, they have a few thousand—but in the asymmetry in the threat perception. The United States does not perceive any threat from our immediate neighbors, Canada and Mexico, whereas Russia perceives significant threats from several countries to the south of them, and their tactical nuclear weapons are directed to those threats.

Therefore, because of this asymmetry it's going to be very difficult to address that issue, but I think important to address it.

The other problem that we would have with such a treaty is that in strategic nuclear weapons we have verified agreements we have made by verifying the missiles themselves, which are quite easy to verify, relatively speaking, but in tactical nuclear weapons we don't have that database to begin with. We don't even know, to begin with, how many tactical nuclear weapons they have. So the verification issue is going to be very difficult. It's going to involve a much higher degree of intrusive inspections than we've ever had in the past.

Senator UDALL. Dr. Miller?

Dr. MILLER. If I could just confirm that you are accurate in your recollection. Declaration No. 11 of the Senate resolution of ratification calls upon the President to pursue, following consultation with allies, an agreement with the Russian Federation that would address the disparity in tactical nuclear weapons; and later on, just as Dr. Perry suggested, suggests taking steps to look to improve transparency and improve confidence in numbers as well.

So that is an important objective, just as the Senate, as Dr. Perry, as the National Security Advisor, has said. At this point we believe that the most effective way to pursue that is likely to be seeking a combined agreement that looks at overall numbers, including deployed and nondeployed, strategic and non-strategic or tactical. That is not a final decision, but that's certainly the approach that we have looked at to date.

Senator UDALL. I may be misinterpreting what I've heard, but it strikes me as a little strange that those who had concerns about the treaty, those who may have even, in fact, voted against the treaty, would be critical of attempts to begin to undertake this important mission to reduce the number of tactical weapons. I wouldn't ask you all to comment on that. That's an opinion I'm expressing. But it seems to me that the administration is keeping faith with those promises that were made to begin to do this important work.

I think my time is about to expire, but I want to ask General Kehler just a quick question about the heavy bombers. Under the previous START treaty, literally we take them apart, as I understand, even cutting the fuselages in half. I don't know if that's on the long axis or the short axis. It probably doesn't matter. Either way, they don't fly very effectively after that.

The New START treaty recognizes legitimate non-nuclear missions and allows for the bombers to be made non-nuclear capable. I think maybe that's the term that's used. Can you describe the methods by which the aircraft are modified so they are not able to carry nuclear weapons, and does that restrict, those modifications, the uses for the airplane in other missions and in other capacities?

General KEHLER. Senator, you have to think about the heavy bombers, I think, in three contexts. There are those that are in the boneyard, essentially, that we don't want to have counted against any limits in the treaty, and that we will just take destructive measures to deal with.

Then there is a category of heavy bombers that will be dual-capable, nuclear-capable bombers that will also be available for conventional missions. Then there is a category that we will not have nuclear-capable at all, but will be available for conventional purposes. That's the category I think you're talking about, and in that case we will propose for our own compliance review group a series of steps that we would take that would make it clear that the bomber was not capable of carrying or delivering nuclear weapons, but still retained its full capability as a platform to deliver conventional weapons, to include precision guided weapons that are conventional.

So we haven't gotten to the complete end of that string yet about approvals to represent it that way with the Russians. That's pending and we believe we have a good way to do that that still allows them to be capable for conventional missions.

Senator UDALL. Thank you for that explanation.

Thank you, Mr. Chairman.

Dr. MILLER. Senator, if I could just add very briefly, just to divide that last part into two different parts. As General Kehler said, we're not at the end of the process yet. In particular for the B–52Hs that would be converted to conventional only, which we plan to do, we are still working through exactly how that will be done and have not yet done an exhibition of that to the Russians.

We did do an exhibition of the B–1B bomber because we have been, as General Kehler knows well, undertaking conversions of those to conventional for some time. That first exhibition of the B–1 bomber, that will allow them to be non-accountable, occurred just a few weeks ago.

Senator NELSON. Senator Shaheen.

Senator SHAHEEN. Thank you, Mr. Chairman.

Thank you all very much for being here. I'm sorry I missed your statements, but I do want to begin by—I'm sure you probably referred to this—but by congratulating all of you on your role in passage of the New START treaty. It was an extensive debate in the Senate. I think finally we were able to get the bipartisan support that was required.

It was interesting to me that after support from virtually every living Secretary of State and Secretary of Defense from both sides of the aisle, that it took us so long to get agreement on the treaty. But it's there and I'm delighted and appreciate that now we have new challenges as we begin to implement it.

There was a lot of discussion during that debate about the importance of getting the treaty passed so that we could again resume on-the-ground inspections. Again, I apologize if you've already talked about this in your opening testimony, but can you talk about—I understand the first of these inspections was done in April, and I wonder if you could speak to what we've learned from that inspection. Were there any surprises or did it go about the way we expected?

Dr. MILLER. Senator Shaheen, first thank you for your words about the New START treaty.

The first U.S. inspection was undertaken in April. It was of an SS–19 base, which is a MIRVed ICBM that's kept in silos. I think that I can say that the inspection went about as expected, and I think in an open session, given our expectations about what's discussed in inspections, that that's about all I should say.

I will also note that we've exchanged databases, we've had the first meeting of the Bilateral Consultative Commission to work through the process through which any future debates would be resolved with respect to inspections.

But I think with respect to this one inspection that's probably all I should say.

Senator SHAHEEN. General?

Senator NELSON. Senator Shaheen, by prior agreement, Dr. Perry has to leave at 3:15 p.m. and we're going to give him 5 minutes to summarize anything that he'd like to say. He has to catch a plane. So if you suspend just for a minute, we'll finish that.

Senator SHAHEEN. I'm happy to do that. I'm pleased that Dr. Perry's here.

Dr. PERRY. First of all, I must apologize. I must apologize for this restriction. When I was Secretary of Defense, the answer to the question, when does the plane leave, is when I get there. That's not the answer any more, so I need to be there, and I have to give a talk tomorrow morning in California.

I want to make a few comments, though, in wrapping up, and pointing out that the threats of nuclear weapons to the United States today are in two very different categories. One is the threat that the nuclear weapons could be used by a terror group against us. So the proliferation and nuclear terrorism is one set of threats, and dealing with that set of threats takes a certain set of actions.

In addition to that, we are not yet able to dispense with deterrence. So we have two different requirements we have to meet: maintaining deterrence while at the same time working to decrease this threat of proliferation and nuclear terrorism. So we have to have a balance in dealing with those two.

That has been recognized, I think, since the end of the Cold War. The policy that we had in the Clinton administration, which was really followed before that and since then, but not by the same name, was called "Lead But Hedge." We lead in the reduction of nuclear arms, we lead in programs to prevent the proliferation, but we hedge against adverse political developments by maintaining our deterrence.

That policy was strongly reaffirmed in the NPR. The Strategic Commission which Keith Payne and I were both on, also reaffirmed that, but that was prior to the NPR. I must say I think the NPR got it just right. It said the U.S. goal was to reduce nuclear weapons, but we will not do it unilaterally, we will maintain deterrence.

Secretary Miller can tell you, but I can also affirm, that the President was intimately involved in this NPR and these are his goals, not just the goals of the people who wrote the report.

The hedging has been achieved, I think, very effectively. We have stated that we're going to maintain a safe, secure deterrence and we're going to do that without building new weapons. We're going to strengthen the scientific program at the three laboratories and that is being done. We're going to rebuild the nuclear infrastructure. That is being done. Very substantial requests for appropriations are in for doing that right now.

We have said we were going to increase the stockpile stewardship program, which has been a great success to this date, but is in danger of deteriorating. So the increased funding of that was very important. We said we're going to increase the emphasis on the life extension program.

Those are all commitments that were made in the NPR. Those are substantial commitments, and in my judgment they are being carried out, with the support and enthusiastic support, I might say, of the U.S. Congress. So I think we are striking that balance. But I would say again that part of the balance is leading on this reduction of nuclear weapons and the move to deal with proliferation and nuclear terrorism. I think that is very important also.

So we cannot debate this issue by looking at just one of these goals. We have to look at both of them at the same time and understand that sometimes they're in conflict and we have to strike a balance between them. In my judgment, we have done a very effective job, the administration has done a very effective job, of striking that balance, and I think in as much as the NPR states clearly and explicitly the goals of the administration I think that is the proper test of how they're doing.

You then have to see, are they following up on the commitments in terms of their requests for support? I believe that the requests for support in this field that went in with this last budget does just that, and now it's up to Congress, I think, to pass those requests. From what I hear, I think Congress is likely to do that.

So I'm feeling very good at this stage about meeting these two goals, the lead on the one hand, which I think the President is doing very effectively, but still maintaining that hedge, still understanding this is a dangerous world and we have to maintain the deterrence of a nuclear force.

Other people can testify better than I how well we're doing that. We have General Kehler here today and he can tell you whether or not he feels confident that we're maintaining our deterrence in the face of these changes.

I very much appreciate the opportunity to speak with this committee. I apologize again for my needing to leave a little early.

Senator NELSON. No need to apologize. We're mindful of your time constraints and thank you so very much; not that you need to be, but you are excused.

Dr. PERRY. Thank you very much.

Senator SESSIONS. Dr. Perry, thank you for your work and leadership on the Posture Commission and for your commitment to the United States.

Dr. PERRY. Thank you, Senator Sessions. Questions on the Posture Commission as they come up in the latter part can be answered very ably by Keith Payne, who is a very close colleague of mine and we worked closely together on the Posture Commission. Thank you.

Senator NELSON. Thank you.

Senator Shaheen.

Senator SHAHEEN. Thank you.

I think, General Kehler, you were about to also respond to my question about the inspections.

General KEHLER. I was, Senator. Let me just make two points, if I could. First is, the debate that you described, the conversations on the nuclear issues, were also noted in Omaha. I can tell you that across STRATCOM the feedback that I get is that they very much appreciate the fact that these issues are getting national attention. So I think that was a point that was not lost on them and they're very appreciative of that fact.

Second, I would just expand on what Dr. Miller said. We are committed to implementing the New START treaty. There are many steps that are already under way. We have less than 7 years already, not a lot less but under 7 years, to bring all of the pieces together. Since the treaty entered into force on the 5th of February, we have done the following things.

Dr. Miller mentioned we've done the first New START database exchange. He also mentioned we've done a required exhibition of B–1 bombers. There has been a required exhibition of the Russian road-mobile SS–27 ICBM and launcher. There has been a required exhibition of our B–2A bomber and, as he described, the first of the U.S. New START onsite inspections. In this case, the Russian SS–19 at Kazelsk has also been accomplished.

There's a lot more to do, but I did want to let you know that there is a full range of activities that are already under way in implementing New START.

Senator SHAHEEN. Thank you. I know that we have until 2018 to bring our nuclear force structure into compliance with the treaty limits. Is there the possibility of moving up that timetable in any way?

General KEHLER. Senator, from my perspective we are right now working with the Office of the Secretary of Defense and the Joint Staff to point together and finalize our plans for what our force mixture will look like as we implement the New START treaty. The 1251 report that was submitted to Congress back in the fall and updated again in the fall describes a baseline force structure that has a certain number of submarine-launched ballistic missile launchers associated with it, up to a certain number of ICBMs, up to a certain number of bombers.

We are now working our way through how do we make those balances and tradeoffs in that mixture. We expect that something will go to the Chairman here in the not too distant future. Some of the precursor steps in order to do those force structure—to execute those force structure decisions, like going to single-warhead ICBMs, we will have to, in a budgetary sense anyway, get going sooner rather than later so that we can have all the pieces in place.

So I think what you will see as we sequence these steps, that some things will actually have to begin sooner simply because it will take us a certain number of years to cycle ballistic missile submarines through the wharves, to handle the weapons, do the things that we're going to need to do.

Dr. MILLER. Senator, if I could just briefly add to General Kehler's excellent, accurate response, two thoughts. One is that once that timeline is defined the United States under the terms of the treaty, as will Russia, will have flexibility to mix forces should that be required because of a problem in one leg or another of the triad—one of the advantages of sustaining the triad, as we intend to do under the treaty.

The second is I wanted to explicitly acknowledge that the administration remains cognizant of the Senate resolution of ratification, its Declaration No. 5, and it talks about asymmetry in reductions and directs that the President should regulate reductions such that no strategic imbalance endangers the national security interests of the United States. So as we look at this we'll also assess the likely timeline and path for Russian reductions as well.

Senator SHAHEEN. Thank you.

My time has expired, but I actually have to say I was pleased, but a little surprised, to hear how optimistic Dr. Perry was about the commitment to continue to fund all of the requirements for our nuclear arsenal. I'm not quite as sanguine as he is about the continued commitment of Congress to do that, given the current budget debate that we're having. So I may get some time later to ask you to comment on that, but thank you.

Senator NELSON. Thank you, Senator.

Some critics of the administration have suggested that the administration's primary goal is getting to zero nuclear weapons and that this is a shift away from the lead-hedge tradition which we just heard Dr. Perry reference and the need to maintain deterrence. Dr. Payne, do you see the administration continuing with the lead-hedge tradition or not?

Dr. PAYNE. I do. For example, my friend Dr. Miller has provided the NPR of 2010 which I think in general is a very commendable document. It certainly reflects a continuing commitment to the goals of deterrence, assurance, limited defense, and extended deterrence.

On the other hand, it's true that concern has been raised with regard to other voices in the administration which seem to subordinate those traditional goals to the goal of nuclear reductions. Senator Sessions quoted National Security Advisor Donilon's announcement of the forthcoming reviews. We should note that National Security Advisor Donilon stated specifically that the forthcoming nuclear reviews are for the purpose of finding further U.S. nuclear reductions. Other senior administration officials have similarly described the purpose of these reviews as being to facilitate nuclear reductions on the journey toward nuclear zero.

In addition, the administration itself has said that, "for the first time"—and that's a quote—"for the first time," it places atop the U.S. nuclear agenda nonproliferation as an element moving toward nuclear zero. So this isn't a concern that comes out of imagination. It's a concern that comes directly out of the way these goals have been described by some administration officials on some occasions.

So I conclude that what we see is in a sense two competing dynamics within the administration regarding the prioritization of

U.S. goals and the calculation of force requirements. One, as is well and ably presented by Dr. Miller, is committed to sustaining effective strategic capabilities for deterrence, assurance, extended deterrence, and limited defense. The other, however, appears to place top priority on arms control and movement towards nuclear zero in the calculation of force adequacy.

I should note, as Secretary Perry noted earlier, reconciling these two dynamics will be very difficult and ultimately impossible. So the fundamental question, I think, that we're presented with—and Senator Sessions identified this early in this discussion—is with regard to the administration's nuclear reviews, which of these two different views or dynamics with regard to U.S. priorities and requirements will dominate?

My concern and the concerns that have been raised by others who see these competing priorities is that the goal that places priority—or I should say, the approach that places top priority on movement towards nuclear zero and other arms reductions will dominate those considerations and by definition subordinate these other goals that have been consistently supported by U.S. Democratic and Republican administrations for 5 decades.

Senator NELSON. General Kehler, from your perspective are you satisfied that the movement is in the right direction in terms of reduction, and are you concerned that the administration will then begin on its own to reduce the number of warheads unilaterally?

General KEHLER. Sir, I would make two points. The first is, on the force levels that are described in the New START treaty, I don't have any concerns with those force levels at all. I think that Dr. Miller earlier described STRATCOM's role in this entire process and our role really is at the right-hand side of the process. If it starts on the left with presidential guidance, that's refined by both the Secretary of Defense and the Chairman. STRATCOM takes that guidance and does mission analysis, and at the end of that mission analysis process we are able to articulate what from our military perspective we believe are the requirements for both force capability and force capacity.

Based upon the guidance that was used to arrive at the New START treaty, I have no concerns whatsoever. I believe that, given that guidance, that we are capable of achieving our deterrence objectives. I think that remains our role as we go forward. Our role will be to examine alternative guidance packages, if you will, and perform the same kind of mission analysis on those, to describe from our military perspective what the implications of various guidance alternatives might be.

I do see that as our rightful role in the process. I am fully expecting that we will be involved as deeply in this process as the command was in the New START discussions and as it was in the NPR itself. The preliminary, although we haven't seen any official taskings, discussions that we've had with Dr. Miller's office and others lead me to believe that our advice is going to be sought.

Senator NELSON. Dr. Miller?

Dr. MILLER. Mr. Chairman, I will just state for the record General Kehler and STRATCOM's advice is being sought and that will continue to be the case.

Senator NELSON. Thank you.

Senator Sessions.

Senator SESSIONS. Thank you.

Dr. Payne, National Security Advisor Donilon in this speech said that "The New START treaty represents a commitment by the world's two largest powers to the goal of disarmament." Do you think the Russians, by signing this treaty, in any way evidenced an inclination to go to disarmament? How would you assess the state of the Russian mind?

Dr. PAYNE. I would suggest that, based on the various statements from senior Russian officials and senior military officials, both in the lead-up to New START and following the ratification of New START, that the chances of the Russians agreeing to nuclear disarmament are so close to zero that we might as well call them essentially zero.

They identify, that is Russian senior officials, both in the military and on the civilian side, the great value they continue to place in nuclear weapons, including for what we would call here warfighting purposes. They have said specifically that because their conventional forces are in poor shape and not likely to get into better shape for many years to come, that they are deeply reliant on nuclear weapons for their security, and in fact virtually all of the senior Russian officials who have commented—I may have missed some—virtually all of the senior Russian official comments that I've seen with regard to the future of tactical nuclear weapons and reductions of tactical nuclear weapons have in a sense said they're not interested in moving in that direction and certainly not in any time soon.

Senator SESSIONS. I'm sure the administration raised it in the New START negotiations and they faced a stone wall because the Russians refused, and so we acquiesced and focused on the strategic.

Dr. Miller, on what basis does the President's National Security Advisor conclude that the New START treaty represents a commitment to disarmament?

Dr. MILLER. Senator Sessions, if you look at the preamble to the treaty, it notes both parties' commitment to nuclear disarmament over the long term. I think it's fair to say that the reductions in nuclear warheads, in deployed nuclear warheads and strategic delivery vehicles, represent a step in that direction.

Senator SESSIONS. I will just say if the President had said to the U.S. Senate, the New START treaty is a start toward disarmament, I guess it would have caused more concern than we had. This does not strike me as a wise approach and it is part of the concern that I have as we wrestle with these very important issues.

I do feel like that President Bush, George W. Bush, our recent President Bush, unilaterally drew down nuclear weapons substantially. He did not do that pursuant to a treaty, but he made clear he was going to a level, as I understood it, he thought was sufficient for our national security and that we were free to take other action, if necessary, to strengthen that capability to protect our national security. So I'm just worried about this trend.

Dr. Payne, there are other players in the world other than Russia. One of the problems we have is that as we draw down our weapons, it seems to me that China may have an incentive to seek equivalence with the United States, nuclear parity with the United States, as might other countries, frankly. According to the report of the Strategic Posture Commission, the Chinese have some 400 nuclear warheads in their arsenal, and according to DOD China deploys 60 long-range ballistic missiles capable of targeting our Homeland.

How can we know with any certainty how many nuclear weapons the United States needs to maintain in order to disincentivize China to seek nuclear parity with the United States? Is that a concern?

Dr. PAYNE. Senator Sessions, that's one of the very difficult questions that confronts us in all of these areas of deterrence and assurance of allies: how do we know what's going to be necessary 5 years from now or 10 years from now; what will it take, for example, if the occasion arises to deter China or to assure an ally?

That's why in my view—and I know General Kehler concurs with this and I suspect that Dr. Miller does as well—that retaining the flexibility of our force to adapt to changes and the resilience of our forces and force structure to adapt to changes is so important.

I guess the conclusion that I draw on that is no one can give you a number right now and give you any kind of confident prediction that this number will be enough to deter 10 years from now or to assure allies 10 years from now, for the simple reason that threats change and opponents change and conditions change. So the requirements for deterrence and assurance similarly shift and change, and so our force structure needs to be agile and resilient and flexible enough to change with the changing threats.

Senator SESSIONS. Isn't it true that other nations depend on the U.S. nuclear umbrella, that there is a political, psychological dimension to clear and strong nuclear capability, and that as a member of the Posture Commission you were able to ascertain that nations around the world who don't now have nuclear weapons, good civilized nations, become concerned as the United States draws its weapons arsenal down too low?

Dr. PAYNE. Yes, sir. What the Posture Commission learned through a whole series of briefings by senior officials from abroad is that they place enormous value on the U.S. extended nuclear umbrella, and that umbrella is provided for some 30 countries, allies in NATO, Japan, South Korea, Australia, and so on.

So what we learned through that exercise was the high priority that these countries place on the U.S. extended nuclear deterrent for their security, and a number of them suggested to us that they are beginning, were at that time beginning, to be concerned about the credibility of the U.S. extended nuclear umbrella and were potentially concerned that if we drew our forces down too far that the credibility of that extended nuclear umbrella would no longer be sufficient in their eyes. Some of them even suggested if that were the case they were going to have to reconsider their commitment to being non-nuclear states.

I should add that we've heard subsequently senior voices, for example, in Japan have said that the threshold at which point they start becoming very worried about the credibility of the U.S. extended nuclear deterrent is if the United States starts moving down to around 1,000 nuclear warheads. So it strikes me that the number that the New START treaty provides of 1,550 is well above that. But when we start looking at numbers that go potentially well below that, we will be potentially jeopardizing the credibility of our extended nuclear deterrent, as judged by our allies, and they are the ones who judge that.

Senator SESSIONS. The perverse consequence of too much reduction could actually be a proliferation of nuclear weapons in other countries that previously did not feel the need to have them.

Dr. PAYNE. Yes, sir. I think it's widely recognized that the U.S. extended nuclear umbrella, extended deterrence, is one of the most important tools for nonproliferation, and to the extent that it is degraded or rendered less credible we would actually be promoting nuclear proliferation, which obviously runs against one of the highest goals of the Obama administration.

Senator SESSIONS. Dr. Miller, briefly, you wrote in your March 2, 2011, House testimony that: "The lack of transparency surrounding China's nuclear program, their pace and scope, as well as the strategy and doctrine that guide them, raise questions about China's future strategic intentions." As we deal with the proper level of nuclear weapons, don't we need to consider also what may be in China's plans for the future?

Dr. MILLER. Senator Sessions, let me divide the answer into two parts. One is about numbers, which you mentioned earlier, and one is about their doctrine and so forth.

With respect to numbers, the United States and Russia still have 90 to 95 percent of nuclear weapons in the world and that will still be the case after the New START treaty is implemented. We unclassified about a little over a year ago the number of nuclear weapons in the U.S. stockpile, as of now almost a year and a half ago. It was 5,113 in the stockpile plus several thousand awaiting dismantlement. Russia is broadly in the same ballpark.

If the numbers cited about China are correct—and I won't say in this forum what the best estimate is from the Intelligence Community—if those are correct, we're 10 times plus above, and we have not seen anything approaching a rush to parity. Instead, we've seen action by China that's consistent with their stated doctrine of wanting to have the ability to deliver in a second strike a relatively limited number of nuclear weapons.

The second part, with respect to transparency——

Senator SESSIONS. You say there's a lack of transparency as to their pace and scope. I don't know how you can be so confident, with that testimony.

Dr. MILLER. I think if we look out—sir, that's the second part, exactly. If we look out from today into the future, today we would like to understand more about their doctrine. It's true for nuclear, it's true for space and cyber space as well, and we've asked for a strategic dialogue with them on these issues.

As we look to the future and try to understand where they might be going, I think that uncertainty grows and our ability to go forward certainly beyond any next round will depend in significant measure on what China does.

Senator SESSIONS. Thank you.

Senator NELSON. Senator Shaheen.

Senator SHAHEEN. Thank you.

Dr. Miller, the administration, though, has always said that we'll maintain a strong deterrent as long as nuclear weapons exist, right? That's been one of the pillars of this administration's nuclear policy. While I appreciate the dichotomy that's been talked about, in fairness that has been one of the things that the President has said from the very beginning; is that right?

Dr. MILLER. Senator, that's correct, a safe, secure, and effective nuclear arsenal as long as nuclear weapons exist. I also should add that that applies not just to deterrence of attack on the United States, but to deterrence of attack on our allies as well. We have consulted very closely with our allies during the NPR and during the New START treaty and have, in fact, established some new bilateral dialogues with allies to have discussions about both nuclear deterrence and broader elements of deterrence, to ensure that we sustain the effective extended deterrence and assurance of our allies.

Senator SHAHEEN. I know that you mentioned that NATO is soon going to undertake its deterrence and defense posture review. Can you give us some insight into what we would like to see NATO come out with as part of that posture review process?

Dr. MILLER. Senator, let me first note that the deterrence and defense posture review is starting from the premises outlined at the NATO summit, and that includes that NATO will remain a nuclear alliance as long as nuclear weapons exist. So that therefore the purpose of the deterrence and defense posture review, is to examine the appropriate mix of nuclear, conventional, and missile defense capabilities.

So what we would like to do is to ensure that as that takes place that we have the continued principles that have been at the foundation of the alliance, including risk-sharing and burden-sharing, as foundational elements of where we go, and that, just as is the case for the targeting assessment that we've talked about, that we look—while we could look at changes in posture, that we fundamentally look at what's required for effective deterrence and assurance as well.

Senator SHAHEEN. As NATO engages Russia in some of these discussions, what's been the reaction from our allies in the Eastern European countries?

Dr. MILLER. NATO in general and including the Baltic States and Eastern European countries have been particularly concerned about gaining more transparency on the status of Russian tactical nuclear weapons and to ensure that those weapons are under the safest possible security arrangements. So what we've seen in discussions with our allies is encouragement to look to initial steps following New START, even prior to considering reductions that aim at increased transparency, and that continue some of the efforts at improved security that, in fact, the Senate and Congress have supported over the years, including through the Nunn-Lugar program.

Senator SHAHEEN. Thank you.

General, do you want to add anything to that?

General KEHLER. Senator, I would just offer that we understand the relationship between our strategic weapons and the requirements of extended deterrence. We understand that not only the

NATO alliance, but other friends around the world, do rely on that, and we are mindful of that as we go about our force planning.

Senator SHAHEEN. As we're looking at the future of arms control and thinking about China, for example, as Senator Sessions mentioned, and what's happening there, have we begun to engage them at all in the debate about arms control and how they might fit into that, whether they might be willing to consider engaging in arms control talks at any point in the future?

Dr. MILLER. Senator Shaheen, we see that, for nuclear arms control, we see an appropriate next round to be bilateral between the United States and Russia, given that we, as I said, account for 90 to 95 percent of nuclear weapons in the world, even after New START. We have often expressed an interest to have discussions with China sooner rather than later, as Senator Sessions referred to, to particularly look at transparency and to understand how they think about planning, how they think about doctrine, and to have a better sense of where they intend to go also with respect to numbers in the future.

We've seen some signs that the Chinese may be open to strategic dialogue in general and I hope that the nuclear issue will be one of those that they pick up on.

General KEHLER. If I could add to that, my predecessor last fall had a counterpart visit in Omaha with one of the senior Chinese defense officials. We would like to see greater military-to-military contact. Of course, Secretary Gates was in China in January and approached that same issue. We have invited Chinese representatives at lower levels in their military structure to come and participate in our public deterrence seminars, for example, and we will do so again this year.

But we would like to see greater contact, certainly at the military level, with the Chinese. There are some questions about their intent. We are supposed to look at capabilities and it's very hard to understand their capabilities on the surface if you don't understand the intent that goes behind it.

Senator SHAHEEN. This is a topic that I haven't heard raised since I've been here this afternoon. Has there been any reaction from Iran upon the passage of the New START treaty? Have they responded to that? From anybody on the panel?

Dr. MILLER. Senator Shaheen, I have not seen any such reaction. I recall an Iranian reaction to the NPR, which, as you recall, for nuclear doctrine it essentially eliminated what we described as the Iran loophole. So that if a country's not meeting its obligations under the Nuclear Nonproliferation Treaty, then our so-called negative security assurance doesn't apply. They noted that that appeared to affect their posture. From our perspective of encouraging them to meet their obligations, I think that was a positive thing, that they noticed.

Dr. PAYNE. I can add to that, Senator Shaheen, that one of the most recent statements that I've seen coming out of Teheran was to suggest that the current events in Libya show what a mistake it was for Libya to give up its weapons of mass destruction, and the leadership in Teheran says: We take note of that.

Senator SHAHEEN. Thank you.

Senator NELSON. Thank you, Senator.

Senator Shaheen mentioned, and so did my colleague, Senator Sessions, about engaging in conversations with China about nuclear reduction. Given the situation with Pakistan quite apart from the events of this week, but the fact that they're a nuclear power and things are less stable in Pakistan, would it be appropriate for us to begin to engage in discussions there with Pakistan about nuclear reduction? Or would we have to do it in conjunction with Pakistan, India, and the United States?

Dr. Miller, do you have any thoughts about that?

Dr. MILLER. Mr. Chairman, we have offered any assistance that Pakistan might desire with respect to our approach in thinking about the most effective means for strategic of nuclear weapons. I don't believe that we've ever suggested that we should at this point include them in any arms control negotiations.

Senator NELSON. Is there a particular reason not to or is it just it doesn't seem to be the time?

Dr. MILLER. Mr. Chairman, I think that in order to look to take additional steps in the coming years, we've made the judgment that it makes sense to look to, for any formal arms control, a bilateral step that would follow a New START.

I might note that, if I recall correctly, that the Posture Commission also recommended an initial first step, given that the START treaty was expiring, and then to look for further steps after that. We think that more—once you go beyond that point, we need to deal with the questions of the security of nuclear weapons globally, the global lockdown that President Obama has talked about, has more than talked about, has advocated and acted on with the nuclear security summit and our follow-on activities. Our real focus in the near-term in that regard is to ensure the security of nuclear materials worldwide and to have as much possible, and indeed all, fissile materials under the safest possible arrangements.

Senator NELSON. You raise a good question about the security discussions and offers of assistance on the security in Pakistan. On a congressional delegation I think in late 2001, I asked President Musharraf how confident he was that they had the security of all their nuclear weapons under control. After a little bit of thought, he said: "95 percent."

So he remembered that, that discussion. So after when we had the unfortunate occasion of flying nuclear weapons all over the United States unknowingly, the next time I saw him he asked me how confident I was that we had our nuclear armaments, nuclear force, under control. I said: "96 percent." [Laughter.]

But in working on this issue, I think the question that is out there that's bothering my colleague, Senator Sessions, and some others is, is there a plan to just unilaterally bring our numbers down without regard to a bilateral agreement with our Russian counterpart? I think that is the question.

Apparently, Mr. Donilon's comments may have obviously helped trigger this question, but would it be possible to get a statement somewhere along the way that would clarify what his speech was about, because that seems to be what the issue, what has triggered the issue at the level that we're dealing with it right now?

I think we're seeing assurances, we're hearing assurances, and I understand that, but there is written documentation out there that seems to be leading in another direction and causing maybe undue concern, but we don't know that it's undue, and that's, I think, what's truly my colleague's concern.

Dr. Miller?

Dr. MILLER. Mr. Chairman, I will want to state that I read and heard the National Security Advisor's speech differently and I found it entirely consistent with what we had said in the NPR and the idea that we would conduct analysis first of how to sustain effective deterrence and assurance and then look to associated numbers. I will take back the question that you've asked, however.

[The information referred to follows:]

The Nuclear Posture Review (NPR) stated that we would pursue additional reductions in strategic and non-strategic nuclear weapons with Russia and that U.S. objectives in future negotiations with Russia will be based on several factors that together will strengthen: deterrence of potential regional adversaries, strategic stability with Russia and China, and assurance of our allies and partners. This will require an updated assessment of deterrence requirements.

Thus, Mr. Donilon's statement that the Department of Defense's review of U.S. strategic requirements will help shape our negotiating approach to the next agreement with Russia is consistent with the administration's previously stated approach in the NPR.

Senator NELSON. Let's see. I think next would be Senator Sessions.

Senator SESSIONS. I think the National Security Advisor's comments were troubling. I don't think they can be blithely set aside. Having just returned from the Baltics and the Ukraine and Georgia, Dr. Payne, what we heard was a very unease about a concern over tactical nuclear weapons. Apparently, the German foreign minister seems to believe that—we should—I don't know if it's the position of the government, but the foreign minister's view is that tactical nuclear weapons should be drawn down in Europe. I got the great concern that ours should be drawn down; and that these nations are really worried that we might reach an agreement that would make the situation even more precarious for them.

Do you have any thoughts about that, any observations about the dynamics of the 10 to 1 or so advantage that the Russians have on tactical nuclear weapons?

Dr. PAYNE. Yes. The Russian numeric advantage in tactical nuclear weapons that you mentioned is of great concern to some allies. Other allies are less concerned, but some allies are particularly concerned, including allies in the Baltic States. This concern, I think, is increased by the Russian position that Russia will not agree to, in a sense, negotiations or to begin the discussions on tactical nuclear weapons until the United States withdraws its nuclear weapons from Europe. So in a sense they say, we don't want to start talking about this until you've withdrawn yours from Europe.

Of course, the problem with that is that I believe we have very little leverage with regard to the Russians on tactical nuclear weapons now. If we withdraw all of our tactical nuclear weapons from Europe as the starting-out point of discussions, I think that leverage is reduced further. Many of our allies understand this, which is why they're concerned both about the asymmetry in capabilities and also the Russian demands with regard to what would happen before discussions could take place.

Senator SESSIONS. Do you think it would assuage their concerns if the Russians were to drop theirs 20 percent and we dropped ours 20 percent, or the Russians said, well, we'll pull back our tactical nuclear weapons 300 miles from Eastern Europe and not have any there? Would that make them feel any better?

Dr. PAYNE. I would refrain from speaking for our allies, but I suspect it would not make some of them feel any better at all.

Senator SESSIONS. In fact, that's what they expressed to us, is a concern that there might be some sort of agreement reached with the United States and that they would make a token reduction or a token pullback, but it would enhance or certainly not diminish the advantage they have.

Now, Dr. Miller wrote about the lack of transparency surrounding China's nuclear programs, their pace and scope, as well as their strategy and doctrine that guide them. It's a plain fact, is it not, Dr. Miller, that the Chinese are playing hardball on this? They're not wanting to talk with us. General Kehler, they've been willing to come over to the United States to some degree and snoop around and see what they can see, but they're not inviting us to China to tell us what they're doing, and they're being pretty hard-nosed about this, are they not?

Dr. MILLER. Senator Sessions, the Chinese have taken a different approach to thinking about deterrence and have emphasized historically not transparency, but almost the opposite, that for effective deterrence it's useful to have uncertainty on the part of the other party. We have attempted to make the case that, in fact, stable deterrence and stable relations between the United States and China would be strengthened by this type of dialogue.

As I said, while we don't know the answer yet, we've seen some positive signs that they will be willing to engage in a strategic dialogue that may include this, among other issues.

Sir, if I could just add very briefly with respect to NATO, what we said in the NPR was that any decisions about nuclear weapons and NATO would not be undertaken unilaterally by the United States, but any decisions would be taken at NATO by NATO. That is precisely what is going on as we begin this deterrence and defense posture review. It's an opportunity for NATO to come together and to have a conversation about the role of nuclear weapons—I should put that differently—about how—what is the appropriate mix of nuclear and conventional capabilities to continue to sustain effective deterrence over time. The guidance that's come from ministers has explicitly stated, just as mentioned in the New START resolution of ratification, that any further steps, any steps by NATO, have to take account of the disparity with respect to Russia.

Senator SESSIONS. Mr. Chairman, thank you for a good hearing. Thank you for calling this. You've allowed us to air these issues at my request. I feel like you were very forthcoming about that.

These are important issues. I don't pretend to know the answers. I know the President, from all his great skill and talent, has not had the kind of experience in these matters over a period of years. I've been on this committee 14 years and I still feel like I'm pretty much a novice, I suppose, to it. So his repeated statements about what I consider to be an unrealistic goal of going to zero nuclear weapons and his very strong desire to have treaties and agreements with Russia, even causing, I think, the negotiations to not be as rigorous as I would like to have seen with regard to the New START treaty, hopefully it doesn't place us in danger. Hopefully the numbers are something we can be comfortable with. But I've been uneasy about that, and I intend to fulfill what I think my duty is to ensure we're thinking clearly, realistically, about the threats we face, the nature of the world in which we live. It's not where we would like it to be. It is the world that is and we have to live in that real world. So I am uneasy about it.

I will probably submit some written questions, but I to date am hopeful that the new funding that the President has supported and Congress seems willing to support will put us on the road for first time in a number of years to see us reconstitute or refurbish our commitments and nuclear capabilities. So that's good news.

I thank each of you for your service to your country very much.

Senator NELSON. Thank you, Senator.

Senator Shaheen.

Senator SHAHEEN. Thank you, Mr. Chairman. I don't have any further questions, but on the NATO discussion I would like to just point out that all of our NATO allies came out very strongly in support of passing New START, and one of the strongest statements came from Poland. So I think, while I appreciate some of the issues that have been raised about next steps, I think it's important to point out that they were very supportive of the passage of the treaty.

Thank you all very much.

Senator NELSON. I want to thank you as well. Thank you, Senator Shaheen, for your service and for being here today; and just to suggest maybe a clarification that might eliminate any confusion that's been raised and discussed during the hearing today.

Thank you all. We're adjourned.

[The prepared statements of Dr. Miller, General Kehler, and Dr. Payne follow:]

PREPARED STATEMENT BY DR. JAMES N. MILLER

Chairman Nelson, Ranking Member Sessions, and members of the subcommittee, thank you for the opportunity to testify today regarding key nuclear issues. I am pleased to meet with you and to testify with the Commander of U.S. Strategic Command, General Robert Kehler; former Secretary of Defense, William Perry; and Dr. Keith Payne.

Just over a year ago, Secretary Gates delivered the 2010 Nuclear Posture Review (NPR) Report to Congress. The NPR provides a roadmap for advancing the administration's comprehensive approach to reducing the role and number of nuclear weapons toward the ultimate goal of a world free of nuclear weapons, while sustaining, as long as nuclear weapons exist, a safe, secure, and effective nuclear arsenal.

We have made substantial progress over the past year in implementing the NPR; our efforts continue, and the Department of Defense (DOD) looks forward to working with Congress to achieve the aims set forth in the NPR. I would like to focus today on five areas in particular: implementation of the New Strategic Arms Reduction Treaty (START) treaty; the revision of presidential guidance; the development of plans for next steps in arms control; the North Atlantic Treaty Organization's (NATO) Deterrence and Defense Posture Review; and the administration's commitment to maintaining a safe, secure, and effective nuclear arsenal.

IMPLEMENTING THE NEW START TREATY

The New START treaty, which entered into force on February 5, 2011, allows the United States to continue to field a credible and flexible nuclear deterrent force. The

Treaty's limit of 1,550 warheads on deployed intercontinental ballistic missiles (ICBM), deployed submarine-launched ballistic missiles (SLBM), and accountable nuclear warheads for deployed heavy bombers allows the United States to sustain effective nuclear deterrence, including sufficient survivable nuclear forces for an assured devastating second-strike capability. The Treaty's limit of 700 deployed ICBMs, deployed SLBMs, and deployed heavy bombers supports strategic stability by allowing the United States to retain a robust triad of strategic delivery systems—while downloading all remaining Minuteman III ICBMs to a single warhead each.

Maintaining each leg of the nuclear triad—ICBMs, SLBMs, and dual-capable heavy bombers—under New START allows us to preserve strategic stability and hedge against any unexpected technical problems or operational vulnerabilities that may arise in any one leg. The administration plans a robust nuclear triad of 700 deployed ICBMs, SLBMs, and nuclear-capable heavy bombers under New START:

- We plan to retain all 14 *Ohio*-class SSBNs and deploy no more than 240 Trident II D5 SLBMs at any time.
- We also plan to retain up to 420 of the current 450 deployed Minuteman III ICBMs, each with a single warhead.
- We plan to retain up to 60 nuclear-capable B–2A and B–52H heavy bombers, while completing the conversion of all nuclear-capable B–1B and some B–52H heavy bombers to conventional-only capability.

DOD is currently defining detailed plans for meeting New START limits. We will give priority to doing so in a cost-effective way over the 7 year implementation period for the Treaty, for example by making any necessary changes to *Ohio*-class SSBNs during their regularly-scheduled maintenance. The Department is committed to providing timely information to Congress as our plans develop further.

A key contribution of New START is its verification regime, which provides a firm basis for monitoring Russia's compliance with its treaty obligations while also providing important insights into the size and composition of Russian strategic forces. The United States and Russia exchanged initial New START databases in March 2011. Required notifications for changes in that data, along with routine updates every 6 months for the entire database, will allow us to track changes in the status of Russian strategic offensive arms covered by the Treaty.

One of the tasks under New START is to remove from accountability hundreds of U.S. strategic delivery vehicles that counted under the old START treaty. This will be done by a combination of offering exhibitions of conventional-only systems including our converted cruise missile-carrying SSGNs and the B–1B bomber, and eliminating a number of ICBM silos and heavy bombers that are no longer in use. The exhibition of the converted B–1B occurred on March 18.

Both Parties have already completed some Treaty-required exhibitions of other strategic systems. The Russian Federation conducted an exhibition of the RS–24 road-mobile ICBM and its associated launcher in March, and the United States exhibited the B–2A bomber in early April.

The Treaty allows each party to conduct up to 18 on-site inspections each year. The United States successfully completed the first of these inspections in Russia on April 16. We expect the Russian Federation to conduct their first inspection soon.

REVISING GUIDANCE

A key part of implementing the 2010 NPR, as with previous such reviews, is the revision of presidential and Departmental guidance for nuclear operations and deterrence, and subsequent modification of operational plans. That effort is now beginning. In follow-on analysis called for in the NPR, DOD will update our assessment of deterrence requirements, including analyzing potential changes in targeting requirements and force postures. Potential changes will be assessed according to how they meet key objectives outlined in the NPR, including reducing the role of nuclear weapons, sustaining strategic deterrence and stability, strengthening regional deterrence, and assuring U.S. allies and partners.

The analysis of potential revisions to guidance and planning will take account of commitments made in the NPR, including:

- Fully implementing New START while retaining and modernizing the triad;
- "De-MIRVing" to single warheads on each ICBM;
- Retiring Tomahawk Land Attack Missile-Nuclear while modernizing Dual-Capable Aircraft and their associated nuclear bomb;
- Fully funding warhead Life Extension Programs and the associated Stockpile Management Program; and

• Making long-deferred investments in the Department of Energy nuclear complex so that it can assure an arsenal of safe, secure, and effective weapons as long as nuclear weapons exist.

The NPR Report reflects clearly the commitment of the Obama administration to ensure that nuclear deterrence remains effective for the problems for which it is relevant in the 21st century. We will continue to ensure that, in the calculations of any potential opponent, the perceived gains of attacking the United States or its allies and partners would be far outweighed by the unacceptable costs of the response. Effective deterrence requires a credible threat to respond. It also requires forces that can put at risk that which a potential adversary's decision makers hold dear.

The analysis will also look at possible changes to force posture that would be associated with different types of reductions. It will consider possible changes to nuclear deterrence strategies associated with changes in the global security environment, as well as the potential contributions of non-nuclear strike capabilities to strategic deterrence. To be well-hedged against geopolitical or technological surprise remains a key priority.

Every President since the beginning of the nuclear age has asked DOD to conduct such analyses and has used that information to inform updated planning guidance to DOD. As Commander in Chief, the President is responsible for determining what is required to protect the United States and our allies and partners, as well as how he wishes the military to support deterrence, to prepare for the possibility that nuclear deterrence might fail, and for taking steps to restore deterrence. Ensuring that our forces are properly sized and configured for the real threats of today and tomorrow is a key responsibility of any administration.

PLANNING FOR NEXT STEPS IN ARMS CONTROL

As stated in the NPR, the United States intends to pursue further reductions in strategic and non-strategic nuclear weapons with Russia, including both deployed and nondeployed nuclear weapons. When complete, the analysis of targeting requirements and force postures will help inform the formulation of any future arms control objectives.

We intend to consider future reductions in the numbers of deployed and non-deployed nuclear weapons, both strategic and nonstrategic, and the associated changes in Russian forces and other variables that would be required to do so in a manner that supports the commitments to stability, deterrence, and assurance.

The NPR noted that because of our improved relations, strict numerical parity between the United States and Russia is no longer as compelling as it was during the Cold War. However, it also noted that large disparities in nuclear capabilities could raise concerns on both sides and among U.S. allies and partners, and may not be conducive to maintaining a stable, long-term strategic relationship, especially as nuclear forces are significantly reduced. It is therefore important to us that Russia joins us in moving towards lower levels.

Maintaining strategic stability with both Russia and China will remain a key priority in the years ahead. We continue to pursue high-level, bilateral dialogues with Russia and China aimed at promoting more stable, resilient, and transparent strategic relationships. Such discussions are moving forward with Russia, and we are seeking similar discussions with China.

It is our intention to keep the Senate fully informed about new developments in U.S. arms control policy and strategy.

CONDUCTING NATO'S DETERRENCE AND DEFENSE POSTURE REVIEW

The 2010 NPR stated that any changes in NATO's nuclear posture should only be taken after a thorough review within—and decision by—the Alliance. We and our NATO allies agreed to conduct a review of NATO's deterrence and defense posture at the Lisbon summit last December. At that summit, leaders approved a new Strategic Concept for the alliance, agreed to update allied capabilities to ensure that allies can make good on Article 5 commitments in the face of new threats, and rejuvenated the alliance's relationship with Russia.

The new Strategic Concept repeats the alliance's traditional formulation that it will maintain an "appropriate mix" of capabilities, both nuclear and conventional, for deterrence and defense. Allies also endorsed territorial missile defense as an alliance mission, thereby reinforcing the interest in determining the appropriate mix in current circumstances.

Accordingly, the primary aim of the Deterrence and Defense Posture Review (DDPR) is to determine the appropriate mix of nuclear, conventional, and missile defense forces that NATO will need to deter and defend against threats to the Alliance and ensure its members' security. The review will also consider how political instruments like arms control can affect the level of capabilities that will be needed in the future and what additional capabilities may need to be created.

The DDPR will be guided by the new NATO Strategic Concept, which states that "[d]eterrence, based on an appropriate mix of nuclear and conventional capabilities, remains a core element of our overall strategy," and that "[a]s long as nuclear weapons exist, NATO will remain a nuclear alliance." The Strategic Concept also notes that the Alliance "will seek to create the conditions for further [nuclear] reductions in the future," and consistent with Senate language in the New START resolution of ratification, that any further steps must take into account the disparity between the nonstrategic (tactical) nuclear weapons stockpiles of the Russian Federation and of the United States.

The DDPR report will be prepared by the North Atlantic Council, where permanent representatives to NATO will work in close consultation with allied capitals to ensure a result that is focused on the requirements of maintaining an effective deterrence and defense posture. We expect that this review will be conducted over the coming year and concluded in spring 2012.

INVESTING IN A SAFE, SECURE, AND EFFECTIVE NUCLEAR ARSENAL

The 2010 NPR highlighted the importance of sustaining a safe, secure, and effective nuclear deterrent. The administration's fiscal year 2012 budget reflects our commitment to the modernization of our nuclear arsenal for the long term, including some $125 billion over the next 10 years to sustain our strategic delivery systems, and about $88 billion over the same period to sustain our nuclear arsenal and modernize infrastructure. These are large investments, but essential to U.S. national security.

As articulated in the NPR and consistent with the New START treaty, the administration is committed to modernizing the nuclear triad:

- Funding began for the *Ohio*-class replacement SSBN in fiscal year 2010 to support the fiscal year 2019 lead ship procurement. Continued research, development, technology, and engineering investments are included in the fiscal year 2012 President's budget request.
- The Navy plans to sustain the Trident II D5 missile, carried on the *Ohio*-class SSBN, through at least 2042 with a robust life extension program.
- The preparatory analysis for a follow-on ICBM capability to be fielded in the 2030 timeframe has begun.
- DOD will continue to maintain heavy bombers to provide a long-range air-delivered conventional and nuclear attack capability for the indefinite future, including upgrades to the B–2 and the development and fielding of a new long-range, nuclear-capable penetrating bomber starting in fiscal year 2012.
- In addition, DOD is developing a new dual-capable Long-Range Standoff missile to replace the current air-launched cruise missile in the latter half of the 2020s.

The NPR identified a number of NNSA nuclear weapons facilities that are decades old and must be replaced or modernized to ensure the reliability of a smaller nuclear arsenal. Two particularly critical facilities are the Chemistry and Metallurgy Research Replacement (CMRR) Facility and the Uranium Processing Facility (UPF), which will take more than a decade to complete. The CMRR and UPF are in their early design phases today; as their designs proceed, we will have more accurate estimates of their costs.

CONCLUSION

A key premise of the 2010 NPR—following the advice of the Congressional Commission on the Strategic Posture of the United States—is that a successful long-term national approach for reducing nuclear dangers must be balanced, with movement in one area enabling and reinforcing progress in other areas. The approach must also be integrated, both nationally—across Federal agencies and between the executive and legislative branches—and internationally among a wide range of partner governments. An effective approach must be sustained over time, with support from a long succession of U.S. administrations and Congresses. A balanced, integrated, and sustained approach to nuclear policy will require a strong bipartisan consensus. This administration has devoted significant time and energy to this effort and we are gratified at the many signs of progress in this regard. Thank you for the opportunity to testify on these critical issues today, and I look forward to your questions.

PREPARED STATEMENT BY GEN. C. ROBERT KEHLER, USAF

Thank you Senator Nelson, Senator Sessions, and members of the Subcommittee for inviting me to join you today to share my views, as the Commander of U.S. Strategic Command (STRATCOM), on several issues that I believe are important to the security of our Nation, our allies and partners, and the world. I appreciate this opportunity to join Dr. James N. Miller, Principle Deputy Under Secretary of Defense (Policy), in discussing the implementation of the New Strategic Arms Reduction Treaty (New START) and the Nuclear Posture Review (NPR). I look forward to describing STRATCOM's role in the implementation of these efforts, to include the follow-on analysis called for in the 2010 Nuclear Posture Review and mentioned by National Security Advisor to the President, Thomas E. Donilon, in formal remarks delivered to the Carnegie International Nuclear Policy Conference on March 29, 2011.

U.S. STRATEGIC COMMAND'S NUCLEAR RESPONSIBILITIES

Before addressing STRATCOM's role in NPR and New START implementation, I would like to describe the roles and responsibilities that STRATCOM is assigned in the execution of the Nation's nuclear strategy.

STRATCOM is assigned combatant command responsibility for the Nation's triad of strategic nuclear deterrent forces: our ballistic missile submarines, intercontinental ballistic missiles (ICBMs), and nuclear-capable heavy bombers, along with the supporting strategic warning, command, control, communications, and planning capabilities. STRATCOM operates these responsive, flexible, and capable strategic forces 24 hours per day, 365 days per year as directed by the President's strategic guidance. While the international security environment has changed dramatically since the end of the Cold War, the purpose of the nuclear deterrent force remains clear: to deter nuclear attack, to assure our allies and friends, and to respond appropriately if deterrence fails. The men and women assigned to STRATCOM perform an essential, and mostly uncelebrated, service to the Nation. It is a service that few Americans think about but all benefit from. As Secretary of Defense Robert M. Gates has said, these men and women and their partners throughout the Departments of Defense and Energy, including the national labs, underwrite the security of the United States as well as our partners and allies.

STRATCOM is also responsible for building the Nation's nuclear employment plans. These plans bolster deterrence by providing the President with credible nuclear response options to achieve his objectives should deterrence fail. All nuclear employment planning is performed in strict accordance with planning guidance transmitted to STRATCOM in three forms: Presidential guidance, Secretary of Defense guidance, and Chairman of the Joint Chiefs of Staff guidance. Each level articulates the President's intent in more detail. Once STRATCOM receives the totality of guidance, we conduct extensive mission analysis to determine the means to achieve the assigned objectives. The resulting plans provide the President with an array of executable nuclear force options. We also maintain a robust adaptive planning capability should circumstances develop in which the President requires options not provided in already built plans.

As the STRATCOM Commander, I am assigned important roles in the broader nuclear enterprise as well. I am a member of the Nuclear Weapons Council. I am responsible for annually certifying to the President the surety of the Nation's nuclear weapons stockpile. I am also responsible for advocating for nuclear force capabilities within the Defense Department. Lastly, I provide professional military advice to the President, the Secretary of Defense, and the Chairman of the Joint Chiefs of Staff on nuclear strategy, operations, and weapons issues.

Given the magnitude of these nuclear responsibilities and the continuing importance of nuclear weapons in our national security posture, STRATCOM's number one priority remains to ensure a safe, secure, and effective nuclear deterrent force.

Of course, the Nation's deterrence toolkit is not limited to our nuclear forces. A potential adversary contemplating a military attack on the United States or our allies and partners needs to take into account the full array of military capabilities at the President's disposal. Particularly important are our ongoing efforts to enhance our regional deterrence architectures through deployment of ballistic missile defenses, advanced conventional precision strike capabilities, and improved abilities to counter weapons of mass destruction. STRATCOM plays important roles in all three of these areas, and we are fully engaged in assisting with the integration of these capabilities in our deterrence strategy and posture.

U.S. STRATEGIC COMMAND'S ROLE IN NEW START IMPLEMENTATION

Let me turn now to the STRATCOM role in implementing New START. STRATCOM played an important and integral role in providing analysis and advice to the team that developed the U.S. negotiating positions. STRATCOM also supported the U.S. delegation when requested throughout the talks and provided advice to both the Secretary of Defense and Chairman of the Joint Chiefs of Staff. STRATCOM's expertise in nuclear strategy, planning, and operations is a unique and invaluable resource.

New START has now entered into force, and the United States has until February 2018—a little less than 7 years—to bring our nuclear force structure into compliance with treaty limits. That may seem like a long time, but much work must be done, and STRATCOM has a leadership role for implementation planning. We are working with the Office of the Secretary of Defense, the Joint Staff, and the Services to determine how we will implement specific provisions of the treaty efficiently and without undue impact on ongoing operations, what resources are required to execute that implementation, and how we will phase and synchronize the implementation steps. The planning is in its initial stages, pending important force structure decisions, consistent with the NPR and 1251 Report, that have strategic, operational, and funding implications. I expect those decisions to be made soon.

Let me make two final points about New START implementation. First, the treaty allows us the operational flexibility to adjust our force structure under its limits to address planned and unexpected events. For example, when combined with a smaller, sustainable weapon stockpile, we can adjust triad warhead loading to meet both near-term needs and potential unforeseen circumstances. This operational flexibility is important for our technical and geopolitical hedging strategy. Second, it is critically important to proceed with the planned investments in force sustainment, force modernization, warhead life extension, Stockpile Management Program, and the Department of Energy's nuclear weapons complex.

U.S. STRATEGIC COMMAND'S ROLE IN NPR IMPLEMENTATION: FOLLOW-ON ANALYSIS

As called for in the Nuclear Posture Review, the Department of Defense will conduct follow-on analysis to update our assessment of deterrence requirements and inform administration thinking about potential future nuclear reductions below the levels in New START. The President will soon direct a strategic force analysis that will develop options for further reductions in our current nuclear stockpile. While STRATCOM has not yet received any formal tasking, I would like to make several points on how I believe our nuclear force requirements should be determined.

I believe a fundamental principle of national security planning is that strategy should drive force requirements, and not vice versa. Stated slightly differently, the "ends" and "ways" of our strategy should determine the required "means" that our forces must provide. The New START negotiating position was based on this fundamental principle. I expect that the follow-on analysis will be based on the same concept: first define the strategy, and then we can determine the force requirements to implement it.

Based on this principle, STRATCOM will have, in my view, two proper roles in the strategic requirements analysis. First, I will provide my best military advice for shaping potential changes in targeting requirements consistent with the principles stated in the Nuclear Posture Review. Second, as the command responsible for conducting strategic nuclear planning and operations, STRATCOM will provide advice on the force structure and force posture required to meet our deterrence requirements.

It is important to note that the Nation's nuclear strategy is broader than just our employment strategy and the force-employment requirements derived from that strategy. Our nuclear forces have always played important strategic functions beyond the classic military role of holding potential adversary target sets at risk. For example, as we consider further negotiated reductions with Russia in our strategic and nonstrategic nuclear weapons, including nondeployed nuclear weapons, our strategy for hedging against technical and geopolitical surprise must inform our negotiating position. My point is that this is a complex endeavor that will require a multidisciplinary approach.

U.S. STRATEGIC COMMAND'S ROLE IN ADVOCATING FOR NUCLEAR ENTERPRISE SUSTAINMENT AND MODERNIZATION

The NPR validated the role of the nuclear weapon complex and the triad and supported investments to modernize these capabilities. The nation faces a substantive recapitalization challenge that will be a multi-decade effort. While the platforms and systems in service today will remain throughout the life of New START, we must not delay our modernization efforts. Delivery system, warhead, and command and control actions must be completed on schedule to address age-related and performance concerns before operational forces are impacted. The length of our acquisition processes means we must now consider the requirements and develop the options for maintaining confidence in our nuclear deterrent capabilities. As we move to lower numbers, we must continue to make adequate investments in flexible force structure, weapons maintenance, and infrastructure sustainment programs.

The substantial support Congress provided for the President's fiscal year 2011 funding request and continued support of the Presidents fiscal year 2012 funding request are key for the long-term safety, security, and effectiveness of our Nation's nuclear deterrent. These programs are essential for the sustainment and modernization of delivery systems (development of *Ohio*-class SSBN replacement, requirements scoping for follow-on bomber and ICBM), stockpile maintenance life extensions (W76–1, B61, W78), infrastructure recapitalization (Chemistry and Metallurgy Research Replacement-Nuclear Facility, Uranium Processing Facility), crucial naval reactor design activities for the *Ohio*-class SSBN replacement, and command and control architectures including the STRATCOM Headquarters command and control complex.

CONCLUSION

Mr. Chairman, Senator Sessions, and members of the subcommittee, STRATCOM is moving forward to implement New START and the NPR efficiently and effectively, and we stand ready to appropriately and fully participate in the strategic force analysis. Thank you for this opportunity to appear before you, and I look forward to your questions.

PREPARED STATEMENT BY DR. KEITH B. PAYNE

The administration recently announced that it will undertake a review of U.S. nuclear requirements. Ultimately, the answer to the question of "how much is enough?" will be determined by the goals U.S. nuclear forces are expected to serve, the priorities attached to those goals and the standards used to judge their adequacy. For over five decades, those goals have been: (1) the stable deterrence of attacks; (2) assurance of allies via extended deterrence and the "nuclear umbrella"; (3) dissuasion of competitive challenges; (4) defense in the event deterrence fails; and (5) arms control. Democratic and Republican administrations alike have consistently given priority to these national goals, particularly stable deterrence, extended deterrence, and the assurance of allies.

The forces pertinent to these five different goals overlap to some extent, but each also has its own unique requirements. For example, the forces that may be adequate to deter attacks on the United States may not be adequate to assure allies.[1] There also can be competing pressures among these goals. For example, arms control initiatives may be incompatible with force standards for deterrence and assurance. Nevertheless, it is the combination of the requirements needed to support these diverse goals that should set the standards for measuring "how much is enough?"

Measuring the adequacy of U.S. forces in this fashion follows the adage that strategy should drive numbers; numbers should not drive strategy. Of course, other factors such as budget and technical realities will intrude, but we should at least start by linking our definition of overall force adequacy to the standards linked to these goals.

An alternative approach is to start with a level of forces preferred for a specific goal such as arms control, and then mandate that the force requirements for deterrence, assurance, defense and dissuasion conform to those preferred arms control levels. The downside of this approach is that the number and types of forces preferred for arms control purposes may ultimately be out of step with those needed to deter, assure, defend and dissuade—in which case, trade-offs must be made at the expense of these goals.

The most fundamental question with regard to the forthcoming review of U.S. nuclear force requirements is what goal or set of goals will take precedence when the administration sets the standards to measure the value and adequacy of U.S. forces.

---

[1] The different requirements for deterrence and assurance were best illustrated by Denis Healey, Britain's Defence Minister in the late 1960s, when he said that, "it takes only 5 percent credibility of American retaliation to deter the Russians, but 95 percent credibility to reassure the Europeans." Denis Healey, The Time of My Life (London: Michael Joseph, 1989), p. 243.

The Obama administration has committed to sustaining effective capabilities for deterrence, assurance and limited defense, and has stated that force reductions must serve the goals of deterrence and assurance.[2] It also has stated that, "for the first time" it places "atop the U.S. nuclear agenda" international nonproliferation efforts "as a critical element of our effort to move toward a world free of nuclear weapons."[3] This prioritization has led to the concern that the goal of nuclear reductions will take precedence in the calculation of "how much is enough?"—particularly when trade-offs must be made.

This concern was stoked when National Security Advisor Thomas Donilon announced the forthcoming nuclear reviews in the context of a conference and speech devoted to the administration's arms control agenda and stated specifically that the nuclear reviews are for the purpose of further U.S. nuclear reductions.[4] Under Secretary of State Ellen Tauscher similarly described the purpose of these reviews— to facilitate nuclear reductions on the "journey" toward nuclear zero.[5]

As described, this approach to reviewing U.S. nuclear requirements poses two serious problems: (1) it starts with the answer that further nuclear reductions are warranted; and (2) it says little or nothing about linking the standards of adequacy for U.S. forces to deterrence, assurance, defense and dissuasion as priority goals.

If the priority goal behind the measure of U.S. nuclear forces is their reduction and ultimate elimination, then other goals such as deterrence, assurance and defense will be subordinated and further nuclear reductions inevitably will be acceptable—if the priority goal is so limited, no other answer could be expected. The conclusions reached on this basis, however, would force our strategies for deterrence, assurance, defense and dissuasion to conform to the lowered force levels deemed desirable for the different goal of further reducing nuclear weapons. That forced fit could undercut our traditional goals of deterrence, assurance and defense.

The administration's apparent willingness to force that fit may be seen in its 2010 rejection of any new U.S. nuclear warheads to support new military missions or to provide any new military capabilities.[6] This policy direction is intended to promote an arms control agenda, but comes at the potential expense of U.S. capabilities important for deterrence, assurance and defense. While Russia lists the United States as its greatest threat and places highest investment priority on the modernization of its nuclear forces, an administration official reportedly has stated recently that further cuts in U.S. nuclear forces could be made "independent of negotiations with Russia."[7] These policies, actions and statements suggest that some in the administration are willing to give precedence to the goal of arms reductions in the critical definition of U.S. force adequacy.

There appear to be two competing dynamics within the Obama administration regarding the prioritization of U.S. strategic goals and the related calculation of force requirements. One generally reflected in the 2010 Nuclear Posture Review is committed to sustaining effective strategic capabilities for deterrence, assurance and limited defense; the other places top priority on arms control and movement towards nuclear zero in the calculation of force adequacy. Reconciling these two dynamics will be increasingly difficult and ultimately impossible absent the transformation of international relations.[8] The fundamental question with regard to the administration's forthcoming nuclear reviews is how these two different views of U.S. priorities and requirements will play out in its calculation of "how much is enough?"

Based on the historical record, we know that U.S. nuclear weapons help to deter war and prevent conflict escalation. We also know that U.S. nuclear weapons help to assure allies and thereby contribute to nuclear nonproliferation. Finally, we know that deterrence can fail and leave us no alternative but to defend. Consequently, we should be wary of any review that does not place priority on the goals of deterrence, assurance and defense.

---

[2] Department of Defense, Nuclear Posture Review Report, April, 2010, p. xi.

[3] Nuclear Posture Review Report, p. vi (italics added); see also p. v.

[4] National Security Advisor Thomas E. Donilon's Remarks at the Carnegie International Nuclear Policy Conference, as Prepared for Delivery and Released by the White House, March 29, 2011.

[5] See the remarks by Ellen Tauscher, Under Secretary for Arms Control and International Security, The Global Zero "GZ/DC Convention," The George Washington University, Washington, DC, April 8, 2011.

[6] Nuclear Posture Review Report, p. xiv.

[7] Desmond Butler, "Promises: Obama's mixed results on nukes," Associated Press, April 5, 2011.

[8] This point is emphasized in William J. Perry and James R. Schlesinger, America's Strategic Posture: The Final Report of the Congressional Commission on the Strategic Posture of the United States (Washington, DC: United States Institute of Peace, 2009), p. xvi.

Various commentators who instead place top priority on movement toward nuclear zero advocate continuing deep reductions—down to levels of 300, 500, or 1,000 warheads—all well below the New START treaty's ceiling of 1,550 warheads. At these much-reduced levels of warheads, they claim the United States could still meet some targeting requirements and thereby retain effective deterrence.

Perhaps, but so subordinating the requirements for deterrence and assurance to the priority goal of further nuclear reductions entails serious potential risks. Most important, the reduced U.S. force posture flexibility and resilience at such low numbers would likely undermine the U.S. capability to adjust to surprising and dangerous political and/or technical developments as may be necessary to deter future wars, assure allies or defend if deterrence fails.

A minimum standard of force adequacy also could make U.S. forces more vulnerable to opponents' covert or deceptive deployments and ease the technical/strategic difficulties for opponents who seek overtly to counter or get around our deterrence strategies— possibly encouraging some to move in these directions. As such, very low numbers could work against U.S. efforts to dissuade nuclear arms competition with countries such as China.

In addition, at minimal force levels the reduced credibility of our extended deterrent would motivate some allies to seek their own independent nuclear capabilities; i.e., it would contribute to incentives for nuclear proliferation among allies and friends and thus be at odds with the administration's stated top priority.

Finally, minimal nuclear force standards and related policies of Minimum Deterrence almost inevitably lead to targeting concepts that seek deterrent effect from threats to kill large numbers of civilians and/or civilian targets.[9] This is because unprotected civilians and civilian targets are highly vulnerable to limited nuclear threats. Successive U.S. administrations have rightly rejected this approach to deterrence as being incredible, immoral and illegal.

These are the primary reasons why, for five decades, Democratic and Republican administrations have rejected a minimum standard for U.S. force requirements and Minimum Deterrence policies—despite their obvious attraction to many in the arms control community. These reasons remain sound.

Is there room for further reductions in U.S. deployed nuclear forces below New START levels because some now suggest that deterrence could be maintained at 300, 500, or 1,000 warheads? The answer must be no, because no estimate of "how much is enough?" for deterrence alone is adequate to understand U.S. strategic force requirements. Recall that U.S. forces also serve the purposes of assurance, dissuasion and if necessary defense. Consequently, no calculation of deterrence requirements—no matter how sophisticated—can define the adequacy of U.S. strategic forces.

Is there room for further nuclear reductions simply because a lower number of nuclear warheads could provide an assured retaliatory capability? The answer again must be no. First, not all U.S. retaliatory threats are likely to be credible. In addition, future threats to us and our allies remain inherently unpredictable in important ways;[10] we will be confronted with unexpected threats because as former CIA Director, George Tenet said, "What we believe to be implausible often has nothing to do with how a foreign culture might act."[11] As a result our deterrence requirements can shift rapidly across time, place and opponent. Consequently, there is much more to the requirements for deterrence and assurance than simply having the number of warheads necessary to satisfy a targeting policy and maintain a retaliatory threat. The requirements for deterrence and assurance include qualitative factors that may be more important than quantity. Particularly critical are the flexibility and resilience of U.S. forces needed to adapt our deterrence strategies to shift-

---

[9] "Likewise, the United States needs relatively few warheads to deter China. A limited and highly accurate U.S. nuclear attack on China's 20 long-range ballistic missile silos would result in as many as 11 million casualties and scatter radioactive fallout across 3 Chinese provinces ... " Pentagon is Exaggerating China's Nuclear Capability to Justify Buying New Generation of U.S. Weapons, Report Finds, Natural Resources Defense Council, Press Release, November 30, 2006. See also, Hans M. Kristensen, et al., From Counterforce to Minimal Deterrence: A Nuclear Policy Toward Eliminating Nuclear Weapons, Federation of American Scientists and The Natural Resources Defense Council, Occasion Paper, No. 7 (April 2009), pp. 2, 31.

[10] As noted recently by both James Clapper and Leon Panetta. See, Leon Panetta, testimony before the House Permanent Select Committee on Intelligence, World Wide Threats Hearing, February 10, 2011; and, James Clapper, testimony before the Senate Select Committee on Intelligence, Hearing, The Worldwide Threat, February 16, 2011.

[11] George Tenet (with Bill Harlow), At the Center of the Storm: My Years at the CIA (New York: HarperCollins, 2007), p. 46.

ing and unforeseen threats and circumstances.[12] This requirement moves the calculation of "how much is enough?" for deterrence alone well beyond a matter of numbers and targeting policies.

Neither I nor anyone else can legitimately claim to know that a much smaller nuclear force would be adequate to deter future attacks and assure allies in the years ahead. Precisely because future threats and the related requirements for deterrence and assurance are so uncertain, it is critical to sustain the flexibility and resilience of our strategic forces necessary to adapt to future, surprising circumstances. Correspondingly, we must sustain the number and diversity of our force posture necessary for its flexibility and resilience—moving to lower force levels than necessary for this purpose would carry real risk.

If we posit that existing U.S. force levels are adequate for deterrence, assurance and defense, the burden of proof must be on those who claim that moving to a dramatically different, lower level of U.S. nuclear forces would continue to provide adequate support for deterrence, assurance and defense. This proof, however, is nowhere to be found because such claims are inherently speculative and typically based on optimistic assumptions about future threats. The inconvenient truth is that no one knows with any level of confidence how many of what types of nuclear forces will be adequate to deter or assure in coming years because threat conditions and opponents can change rapidly. This again is why sustaining the level of U.S. forces compatible with their flexibility and resilience is so critical.

How much risk is reasonable in this regard? Following comprehensive analyses, the former Commander of STRATCOM, General Kevin Chilton, recently concluded that New START force levels would provide adequate force flexibility for deterrence under specific assumed conditions.[13] But, even with optimistic assumptions about the future, Gen. Chilton explicitly cautioned against further reductions below New START force levels.[14] Nothing has changed over the past few months to suggest that Gen. Chilton's caution no longer is valid. To the contrary, recent developments suggest some troubling threat conditions. For example, Russia has demonstrated the great war-fighting value it places on its large arsenal of tactical nuclear weapons, and its 2010 Military Blueprint identifies NATO and the United States as the primary threats to Russia.[15]

In sum, the administration has voiced commitments to U.S. strategic forces and to the goals of deterrence, assurance, and limited defense. But recent statements with regard to the intent behind the forthcoming nuclear reviews cast some doubt on those commitments. If the reduction of nuclear forces en route to zero is the operative top goal of "the U.S. nuclear agenda," then the forthcoming reviews undoubtedly will find a basis for further reductions. Deep reductions, however, would entail significant potential risks, which is why Democratic and Republican administrations for 5 decades have rightly rejected minimalist standards of force adequacy and related minimalist notions of deterrence. These may seem attractive if the "journey" to nuclear zero is the priority that dominates calculations of "how much is enough?"—but not otherwise.

[Questions for the record with answers supplied follow:]

QUESTIONS SUBMITTED BY SENATOR E. BENJAMIN NELSON

IMPLEMENTATION OF THE NUCLEAR POSTURE REVIEW

1. Senator NELSON. Dr. Miller, the administration's Nuclear Posture Review (NPR) formed the basis for the New Strategic Arms Reduction Treaty (START) negotiations, but it is also the basis for the development of the policy documents that will actually implement the NPR. There are three basic documents that need to be

---

[12] Flexibility meaning U.S. possession of a spectrum of possible threat options suitable for a wide range of opponents and contingencies, and resilience meaning the capability to adapt deterrence to changes in threats and contexts, including rapid and unanticipated changes. See, Keith B. Payne, "Maintaining Flexible and Resilient Capabilities for Nuclear Deterrence," Strategic Studies Quarterly (forthcoming, Summer 2011), p. 13.

[13] Gen. Kevin Chilton, Senate Armed Services Committee, Hearing to Receive Testimony on the Nuclear Posture Review, April 22, 2010, pp. 8, 13, 14; and General Kevin Chilton, House Armed Services Committee, Hearing, U.S. Nuclear Weapons Policy and Force Structure, April 15, 2010, p. 11.

[14] Gen. Kevin Chilton, Senate Foreign Relations Committee, Hearing, The New START treaty: Views from the Pentagon, June 16, 2010, Federal News Service.

[15] Aleksey Arbatov, "Arbatov on Need to Balance Army: With Available Resources, Clearer Foreign Policy," Voyenno-Promyshlennyy-Kuryer Online, March 30, 2011, CEP20110330358006.

developed: the presidential guidance; the Secretary of Defense guidance; and the guidance from the Chairman of the Joint Chiefs of Staff. What is the status of each of these documents; what is the process for developing these documents; and why are they important?

Dr. MILLER. Generally, three high-level documents provide overall policy guidance regarding U.S. nuclear weapons.

Presidential guidance provides high-level direction on our nuclear deterrence strategy, employment/targeting policy, and force posture. I anticipate that President Obama will issue new presidential guidance later this year that incorporates many of the policy decisions reached during the NPR.

The Secretary of Defense provides additional guidance in a document known as the Policy Guidance for the Employment of Nuclear Weapons (NUWEP) that implements and amplifies presidential guidance. The NUWEP is an annex to DOD's Guidance for Employment of the Force. The current NUWEP was issued in 2008. It will be revised by the Office of the Under Secretary of Defense for Policy in close coordination with the Joint Staff, U.S. Strategic Command (STRATCOM), the military departments, and other combatant commands following the issuance of the new Presidential guidance, and provided for approval by the Secretary of Defense.

The Chairman of the Joint Chiefs of Staff also issues a document known as the Nuclear Supplement to the Joint Strategic Capabilities Plan (JSCP–N), which provides additional direction to military planners regarding the preparation of contingency plans for potential employment of U.S. nuclear weapons. The current JSCP–N was issued in 2004 and will be revised after the issuance of new presidential guidance and the NUWEP.

2. Senator NELSON. General Kehler, STRATCOM is responsible for building its targeting plans in response to the guidance documents we just discussed. Can you please explain the process by which these targeting plans are developed?

General KEHLER. National-level target planning guidance flows from the President to the Secretary of Defense, then to the Chairman of the Joint Chiefs, and on to STRATCOM. STRATCOM planning begins with an analysis of the national level target planning guidance. The STRATCOM commander translates this guidance into direction for his staff and components through planning directives, guidance statements, and verbal instructions.

To develop detailed targeting plans, STRATCOM develops a target list and then allocates specific weapon types to the targets, based on target characteristics and weapon performance factors. Next, STRATCOM plans specific weapons, down to the specific unit and platform for the targets previously constructed. Finally, the completed plans are approved by the Secretary of Defense, prior to distribution to national decision makers and dissemination to U.S. nuclear forces.

TARGETING AND ALERT POSTURE

3. Senator NELSON. General Kehler, in a speech at the Carnegie Nonproliferation Conference last month, National Security Advisor, Tom Donilon, said that in developing options for future reductions: "we need to consider several factors, such as potential changes in targeting requirements and alert postures." What changes in targeting postures are you considering?

General KEHLER. It is premature to discuss changes in targeting requirements prior to this review.

4. Senator NELSON. General Kehler, what changes in alert postures are you considering?

General KEHLER. The current nuclear alert posture was reaffirmed in the 2010 NPR. Potential changes to that alert posture to be considered in the NPR follow-on requirements review have not yet been identified.

5. Senator NELSON. Dr. Miller, is the Department of Defense (DOD) considering any changes in the alert posture of nuclear forces?

Dr. MILLER. The 2010 NPR examined possible adjustments to the alert posture of U.S. strategic forces and concluded that the current posture—with heavy bombers off full-time alert, nearly all intercontinental ballistic missiles (ICBM) on alert, and a significant number of SSBNs at sea at any given time—should be maintained for the present. Potential changes to alert posture may be considered in the NPR follow-on analysis, and if so, I expect such changes would be assessed by whether they support the NPR goals of maintaining strategic deterrence and stability at reduced nuclear force levels, strengthening regional deterrence, and reassuring U.S. allies and partners.

UNILATERAL DISARMAMENT

6. Senator NELSON. Dr. Miller, I think there is concern that the administration is headed down a path to make unilateral reductions in U.S. nuclear weapons. Is the administration planning to make unilateral reductions or will all future reductions be in the context of bi- or multi-lateral legally binding treaties?

Dr. MILLER. As stated in the 2010 NPR report, the administration will pursue a follow-on agreement to New START with Russia that binds both countries to further reductions in all nuclear weapons. The NPR report noted that while the need for strict numerical parity between the two countries is no longer as compelling as it was during the Cold War, large disparities in nuclear capabilities could raise concerns on both sides and among U.S. allies and partners. Therefore significant disparities may not be conducive to maintaining a stable, long-term strategic relationship, especially as nuclear forces are significantly reduced. Therefore, we will place importance on Russia joining in moving towards lower levels.

It is our intention to keep the Senate fully informed about new developments in U.S. arms control policy and strategy.

7. Senator NELSON. Dr. Miller, when is the right time to bring China, India, Pakistan, or others into discussions with respect to nuclear weapons?

Dr. MILLER. China, India, Pakistan, and others are already part of multilateral discussions on nuclear nonproliferation. This is a key element of the President's "nuclear security agenda." As stated in the NPR report, the administration will pursue a follow-on agreement with Russia that binds both countries to further reductions in all nuclear weapons. This approach makes sense because even after New START, the United States and Russia will still have 95 percent of the world's nuclear weapons. Depending on the degree of any post-New START reductions made by the United States and Russia, it could well make sense to expand the negotiating process to a multilateral approach for subsequent steps.

It is our intention to keep the Senate fully informed about new developments in U.S. arms control policy and strategy.

MAINTAINING THE TRIAD

8. Senator NELSON. Dr. Miller, in the NPR, DOD said that it would maintain the triad of nuclear forces. Is there any discussion or plan to go to a dyad of nuclear forces, and eliminate one of the three legs of the triad?

Dr. MILLER. The triad has significant advantages, and at this time the administration has not changed its stated plan to sustain a triad under the New START treaty. However, given the requirement to identify significant cost savings for DOD over the next decade or more, no set of capabilities can be considered to be completely "off the table." The administration intends to provide a baseline force structure for the New START treaty as part of the fiscal year 2013 budget submission.

―――――

QUESTIONS SUBMITTED BY SENATOR JEFF SESSIONS

FURTHER REDUCTIONS

9. Senator SESSIONS. Dr. Miller and General Kehler, in a recent speech at the Carnegie Endowment, the President's National Security Advisor, Tom Donilon, stated that the administration is currently "making preparations for the next round of nuclear reductions" and that DOD will "review our strategic requirements and develop options for further reductions in our current nuclear stockpile." He continued by stating that in meeting these objectives, "the White House will direct DOD to consider potential changes in targeting requirements and alert postures." With respect to Mr. Donilon's comments, what guidance and assumptions have you been given or told to follow in the design, development, and posture for modernizing the nuclear triad?

Dr. MILLER. At this time, DOD has not received additional White House guidance beyond the President's approval of the 2010 NPR, which included commitments to:

• Implement the New START treaty fully while maintaining the triad;
• "De-MIRV" to a single warhead on each ICBM;

- Retire Tomahawk Land Attack Missile-Nuclear while modernizing Dual-Capable Aircraft and the associated nuclear bomb;
- Fund warhead Life Extension Programs and the associated Stockpile Management Program fully; and
- Make long-deferred investments in the Department of Energy nuclear complex so that it can ensure an arsenal of safe, secure, and effective weapons as long as nuclear weapons exist.

I expect that DOD will receive White House guidance within the next several months for conducting an analysis of options for future targeting requirements and alert postures.

General KEHLER. The administration outlined a long-term approach to nuclear triad modernization and sustainment in both the NPR and 1251 report, and I fully support these plans. Until the NPR follow-on requirements review is conducted, it is not possible to say what—if any—changes will result, but I do expect any changes to be consistent with the findings of the NPR.

10. Senator SESSIONS. General Kehler, have you been asked to conduct any technical analysis on modifications to force structure?

General KEHLER. We have not yet been tasked to conduct any specific, technical analyses for the NPR follow-on requirements review. However, we are participating in studies on the sustainment and modernization of the force, and I expect STRATCOM to be a full participant in the NPR follow-on requirements review.

11. Senator SESSIONS. General Kehler, we were told the balance of forces represented by the New START treaty would be stable and that those force levels were what was necessary to support U.S. deterrence requirements. Why is it necessary to pursue further reductions?

General KEHLER. The NPR recommended the conduct of a follow-on analysis to set goals for future reductions below the levels expected in new START, while strengthening deterrence of potential regional adversaries, strategic stability vis-á-vis Russia and China, and assurance of our allies and partners. The pace and magnitude of potential future reductions should be influenced by the outcome of this analysis, as well as the following:

- Full implementation of the Stockpile Stewardship Program and the nuclear infrastructure investments recommended in the NPR and codified in the 3113 (Stockpile Stewardship and Management Plan) and 1251 reports; and
- Russia joining us as we move to lower levels of nuclear weapons.

12. Senator SESSIONS. General Kehler, in your best military judgment, how prudent is it to begin consideration of reductions past the New START levels?

General KEHLER. It is prudent to consider any actions that have the potential to improve the security of the United States and its allies by enhancing deterrence and maintaining strategic stability. I will always evaluate any such actions carefully and provide my best military judgment accordingly. In the meantime, STRATCOM is fully engaged in implementing the New START treaty.

NUCLEAR DOCTRINE AND TARGETING GUIDANCE

13. Senator SESSIONS. Dr. Miller and General Kehler, why is the administration contemplating changes to well-established nuclear doctrine and targeting requirements?

Dr. MILLER. Over the last 50 years, U.S. nuclear doctrine and targeting strategy have continually evolved with the global strategic environment. Given continued changes globally, the United States would be remiss if we did not reexamine our nuclear strategy and targeting requirements in today's dynamic security environment. As General Kehler stated, DOD routinely conducts analysis to inform nuclear planning. As Commander in Chief, the President is responsible for determining what is required to protect the United States and our allies and partners, as well as how he wishes the military to support deterrence, to prepare for the possibility that nuclear deterrence may fail, and, should that occur, to take steps to end conflict on the best possible terms.

General KEHLER. As discussed in the NPR, the security environment has changed dramatically since the end of the Cold War. A review is a prudent step towards addressing the top priorities discussed in the NPR:

- Discourage additional countries from acquiring nuclear weapons;

- Prevent terrorists from acquiring nuclear weapons or materials to produce them;
- Maintain stable strategic relationships with Russia and China; and
- Counter threats posed by emerging nuclear-armed states.

14. Senator SESSIONS. Dr. Miller and General Kehler, to the extent you can in an unclassified response, please describe current nuclear doctrine and targeting guidance.

Dr. MILLER. Current doctrine and targeting guidance provide the President with a wide range of pre-planned, flexible response options should deterrence fail. Planners are directed to develop response options designed to hold at risk targets that a potential adversary values, while minimizing civilian and other collateral damage, and where possible to limit damage to the United States and our allies and partners. Planners are also directed to provide the ability for "adaptive planning" to provide additional options if directed to respond to unanticipated circumstances. The United States continues the practice of open-ocean targeting of all ICBMs and SLBMs. This is so that in the highly unlikely event of an unauthorized or accidental launch, the missile would land in the open ocean. The maintenance of such flexibility in our forces and planning capability has been a cornerstone of U.S. nuclear policy for decades and will remain a key component of our upcoming analysis.

General KEHLER. U.S. nuclear doctrine can be broadly defined as follows:

- The fundamental role of nuclear weapons, which will continue as long as nuclear weapons exist, is to deter nuclear attack on the United States, our allies, and partners;
- The United States will not use or threaten to use nuclear weapons against non-nuclear weapons states that are party to the NPT and in compliance with their nuclear nonproliferation obligations. In the case of countries not covered by this assurance, a narrow range of contingencies remain in which U.S. nuclear weapons may still play a role in deterring a conventional or CBW attack against the United States or its allies and partners; and
- The United States would only consider the use of nuclear weapons in extreme circumstances to defend the vital interests of the United States or its allies and partners.

15. Senator SESSIONS. Dr. Miller and General Kehler, what is wrong with the current guidance?

Dr. MILLER. Current guidance is not "wrong." Over the last 50 years, U.S. nuclear doctrine and targeting strategy have continually evolved with the global strategic environment. The United States would be remiss if we did not reexamine our nuclear strategy in today's dynamic security environment. Revisions to current guidance may be required to ensure that our forces remain properly sized and configured for the real threats of today and tomorrow. Updating guidance to support deterrence is a key responsibility of any administration and both previous NPRs preceded presidential updates in nuclear guidance.

General KEHLER. Reviewing nuclear employment guidance following a NPR is a logical follow-on step, given past precedent and today's dynamic security environment.

16. Senator SESSIONS. Dr. Miller and General Kehler, has there been a change in global security conditions that warrants a guidance change?

Dr. MILLER. Since the last NPR was completed in 2001, global security conditions have changed significantly. We would be remiss if we did not review nuclear guidance rigorously and review it as needed.

General KEHLER. As noted in the NPR, there have been significant and ongoing changes in global security conditions. The purpose of the NPR follow-on requirements review is to determine whether, and in what ways, those changes might require changes in guidance.

17. Senator SESSIONS. Dr. Miller and General Kehler, what will be the impact of these changes on our ability to assure our allies?

Dr. MILLER. As noted in the 2010 NPR Report, reassuring U.S. allies and partners is one of the key objectives of U.S. nuclear deterrence policies. Any changes in our nuclear posture which supports these policies will be considered in the context of our continuing need to assure our allies and partners of our commitment to their security. It is the administration's goal to demonstrate this commitment not only through words, but also by tangible deeds and capabilities.

General KEHLER. Until we receive and begin to review any updated guidance, it is premature to speculate on the impact of potential changes. However, consistent with the NPR, any potential changes to our employment guidance will be evaluated regarding their impacts on our ability to assure our allies in the context of global security conditions.

18. Senator SESSIONS. Dr. Miller and General Kehler, what will be the impact of these changes on our ability to discourage other countries from seeking strategic equivalence with the United States in nuclear weapons?

Dr. MILLER. Russia is the only country that maintains nuclear forces in numbers that are on par with the United States. While noted in the 2010 NPR Report, the need for strict numerical parity between the two countries is no longer as compelling as it was during the Cold War, large disparities between the nuclear capabilities of the United States and Russia could raise concerns on both sides, and among U.S. allies and partners, and jeopardize the prospect for further reductions. Therefore, we will place importance on Russia joining us as we move to lower levels. Remaining well-hedged against both technological and geopolitical surprise (e.g., an attempted "sprint to parity" by a third country) remains a key priority and is one of the metrics we intend to use to assess any potential changes in our nuclear doctrine and force structure.

General KEHLER. Until we receive and begin to review any updated guidance, it is premature to speculate on the impact of potential changes. However, consistent with the NPR, any potential changes to our employment guidance will be evaluated regarding their impacts on our ability to discourage other countries from seeking strategic equivalence with the United States in nuclear weapons.

19. Senator SESSIONS. Dr. Miller and General Kehler, what will be the impact of these changes on our ability to hedge against future threats and uncertainties?

Dr. MILLER. Remaining well-hedged against geopolitical or technological surprise will be a key metric by which we intend to assess any potential changes in U.S. nuclear doctrine or force structure.

General KEHLER. Until we receive and begin to review any updated guidance, it is premature to speculate on the impact of potential changes. However, consistent with the NPR, any potential changes to our employment guidance will be evaluated regarding their impacts on our ability to hedge against future threats and uncertainties.

ALERT POSTURE

20. Senator SESSIONS. Dr. Miller and General Kehler, why did Mr. Donilon suggest a need to re-review our alert posture?

Dr. MILLER. The 2010 NPR examined possible adjustments to the current alert posture of U.S. strategic forces and concluded that the current posture should be maintained for the present. However, the NPR also directed the initiation of studies that could lead to future reductions in alert posture, including potential new modes of basing for ICBMs that may ensure the survivability of this leg of the triad while eliminating or reducing incentives for prompt launch.

DOD continually assesses our deterrence requirements, including potential changes in targeting requirements and alert postures that are required for effective deterrence. We expect that the NPR follow-on analysis will consider postures that offer varying degrees of flexibility and redundancy with respect to our deterrence and related targeting objectives, and identify the force levels needed to support those objectives and any potential risks associated with each.

This approach is entirely consistent with Mr. Donilon's statement that the DOD's review of U.S. strategic requirements will help shape our negotiating approach to the next agreement with Russia.

General KEHLER. Mr. Donilon stated his rationale for re-review in his 2011 Carnegie International Policy Conference speech. The NPR concluded "that the current alert posture of U.S. strategic forces—with heavy bombers off full-time alert, nearly all ICBMs on alert, and a significant number of SSBNs at sea at any given time—should be maintained for the present." The NPR went on to state: "Looking into the longer term, NPR initiated studies may lead to future reductions in alert posture. For example, in an initial study of follow-on systems to the Minuteman III ICBM force, the DOD will explore whether new modes of basing may ensure the survivability of this leg of the triad while eliminating or reducing incentives for prompt launch."

21. Senator SESSIONS. Dr. Miller and General Kehler, didn't the NPR from just a year ago conclude that the current alert posture should be maintained?

Dr. MILLER. You are correct. The 2010 NPR examined possible adjustments to the current alert posture of U.S. strategic forces and concluded that the current posture should be maintained for the present. However, the NPR also directed the initiation of studies that over the longer term may lead to future reductions in alert posture. For example, an initial study to explore whether new modes of basing for ICBMs may ensure the survivability of this leg of the triad while eliminating or reducing incentives for prompt launch. We live in a highly dynamic security environment. The purpose of the NPR follow-on analysis is to ensure that our forces remain properly configured for the real threats of today and tomorrow.

General KEHLER. Yes.

22. Senator SESSIONS. Dr. Miller and General Kehler, what is destabilizing about the current alert posture?

Dr. MILLER. The 2010 NPR report recommended that the current alert posture of U.S. strategic forces—with heavy bombers off full-time alert, nearly all ICBMs on alert, and a significant number of SSBNs at sea at any given time—should be maintained for the present. However, the NPR report also stated that the United States should continue to posture U.S. forces and enhance command and control arrangements for strategic nuclear forces to reduce further the possibility of nuclear launches resulting from accidents, unauthorized actions, or misperceptions, while maximizing the time available to the President to consider whether to authorize the use of nuclear weapons. We live in a highly dynamic security environment. The purpose of the NPR follow-on analysis is to ensure that our forces remain properly sized and configured for the real and evolving threats of today and tomorrow.

General KEHLER. The NPR reaffirmed the current alert posture. In my view, our current alert posture is not destabilizing. We are constantly reviewing our alert posture to see if it may be possible to make changes that further enhance our security without increased risk.

23. Senator SESSIONS. Dr. Miller and General Kehler, are U.S. forces on hair trigger alert?

Dr. MILLER. Although it is true that portions of the U.S. nuclear triad are capable of rapid execution upon authorization from the President, a robust system of safeguards and procedures is in place to prevent the accidental or unauthorized launch of a U.S. nuclear weapon. These safeguards and procedures have been successful for many decades and we continually refine them to ensure their continued effectiveness.

The 2010 NPR examined possible adjustments to the current alert posture of U.S. strategic forces and concluded that the current posture—with heavy bombers off full-time alert, nearly all ICBMs on alert, and a significant number of SSBNs at sea on alert at any given time—should be maintained for the present. It also stated that the United States should continue to posture U.S. forces and enhance the command and control architecture for strategic nuclear forces to minimize the possibility of nuclear launches resulting from accidents, unauthorized actions, or misperceptions, while maximizing the time available for the President to consider whether to authorize the use of nuclear weapons. The net result of the U.S. alert posture should remain that any potential adversary must conclude that the gains for initiating nuclear hostilities against the United States would be far outweighed by the costs, which is the essence of deterrence.

General KEHLER. Although it is true that portions of the U.S. nuclear triad are capable of rapid execution upon authorization from the President, a robust system of safeguards and procedures is in place to prevent the accidental or unauthorized launch of a U.S. nuclear weapon. These safeguards and procedures have been successful for many decades and we continually refine them to ensure their continued effectiveness.

The 2010 NPR examined possible adjustments to the current alert posture of U.S. strategic forces and concluded that the current posture—with heavy bombers off full-time alert, nearly all ICBMs on alert, and a significant number of SSBNs at sea on alert at any given time—should be maintained for the present. It also stated that the United States should continue to posture U.S. forces and enhance the command and control architecture for strategic nuclear forces to minimize the possibility of nuclear launches resulting from accidents, unauthorized actions, or misperceptions, while maximizing the time available for the President to consider whether to authorize the use of nuclear weapons. The net result of the U.S. alert posture is that any potential adversary must conclude that the gains for initiating nuclear hostilities against the United States would be far outweighed by the costs, which is the essence of deterrence.

24. Senator SESSIONS. Dr. Miller and General Kehler, what are the risks of further de-alerting U.S. nuclear forces?

Dr. MILLER. The 2010 NPR examined possible adjustments to the current alert posture of U.S. strategic forces and concluded that the current posture—with heavy bombers off full-time alert, nearly all ICBMs on alert, and a significant number of SSBNs at sea on alert at any given time—should be maintained for the present. The 2010 NPR report also concluded that reducing the alert rates for ICBMs and at-sea rates of SSBNs could reduce crisis stability by giving an adversary the incentive to attack before re-alerting was complete.

However, the NPR report also stated that the United States would study potential changes that could lead to future reductions in alert posture, such as alternate basing modes for ICBMs. In addition, the NPR report affirmed that the United States should continue to posture U.S. forces and enhance command and control arrangements for strategic nuclear forces to reduce further the possibility of nuclear launches resulting from accidents, unauthorized actions, or misperceptions, while maximizing the time available to the President to consider whether to authorize the use of nuclear weapons. We live in a highly dynamic security environment. The purpose of the NPR follow-on analysis is to ensure that our forces remain properly sized and configured for the real threats of today and tomorrow.

General KEHLER. Any relaxation of alert posture must consider the effect of these actions on the geopolitical environment, our ability to achieve national objectives, and the corresponding actions taken by other nuclear powers. Potential risks and benefits are scenario-specific but could include crisis stability concerns as forces are re-alerted.

25. Senator SESSIONS. Dr. Miller and General Kehler, wouldn't these risks be destabilizing during a crisis as each side starts to re-alert its forces?

Dr. MILLER. The 2010 NPR concluded that reducing the alert rates for ICBMs and at-sea rates of SSBNs could reduce crisis stability by giving an adversary the incentive to attack before re-alerting was complete. The 2010 NPR concluded that the current posture—with heavy bombers off full-time alert, nearly all ICBMs on alert, and a significant number of SSBNs at sea on alert at any given time—should be maintained for the present.

However, the NPR report also stated that the United States would study potential future changes that could lead to reductions in alert posture, such as alternate basing for ICBMs. In addition, the NPR report stated that the United States should continue to posture U.S. forces and enhance command and control arrangements for strategic nuclear forces to reduce further the possibility of nuclear launches resulting from accidents, unauthorized actions, or misperceptions, while maximizing the time available to the President to consider whether to authorize the use of nuclear weapons. We live in a highly dynamic security environment. The purpose of the NPR follow-on analysis is to ensure that our forces remain properly sized and configured for the real threats of today and tomorrow.

General KEHLER. Any relaxation of alert posture must consider the effect of these actions on the geopolitical environment, our ability to achieve national objectives, and the corresponding actions taken by other nuclear powers. Potential risks and benefits are scenario-specific but could include crisis stability concerns as forces are re-alerted.

STRATEGIC BALANCE

26. Senator SESSIONS. Dr. Payne, as I mentioned in my opening comments, I am concerned this administration intends to ignore the importance of achieving strategic balance and establishing a defensive posture that is neither overly reliant nor overly abolitionist towards nuclear deterrence, opting instead for a political agenda focused on unilateral reductions. Do you agree that pursuing unilateral reductions is a risky proposition?

Dr. PAYNE. On June 1, 2011, the Department of State released the first data exchange on U.S. and Russian strategic forces under the New START. That data exchange demonstrates conclusively that Russia's deployed forces were below the treaty's ceiling on the first day the treaty came into force. In contrast, the United States will have to make reductions in its deployed warheads and launchers. Consequently, New START does indeed require unilateral U.S. reductions, a fact long-denied by senior Obama administration officials. These unilateral reductions that follow from

U.S.-Russian negotiations and treaty-imposed limits on U.S. forces are different from unilateral U.S. decisions to reduce its forces as appropriate to ensure that U.S. forces are compatible with U.S. requirements and potential requirements.

If the United States unilaterally adjusts its forces and in doing so maintains all of the forces necessary to meet the spectrum of goals those forces are intended to support, then unilateral reductions will not necessarily pose a risk. However, if those reductions are mandated by negotiated treaty ceilings and other legal constraints that impose enduring boundaries on current and future U.S. force options, then the great risk is that those reductions and limits will prevent the United States from fielding the number and types of forces that may be necessary now and in the future to help deter war, assure worried allies, and defend against attacks, if necessary. In addition, such unilateral reductions preclude one of the preeminent values attributed to arms control negotiations, i.e., securing some degree of our desired reductions in an opponent's forces in return for accepting to some degree its desired reductions in our forces. (Indeed, the Obama administration presented the major value of New START in terms of the reductions it supposedly imposed on deployed Russian forces.) The great risk of our engaging in unilateral reductions as part of a negotiated agreement is that the United States effectively gives up the negotiating leverage that otherwise resides in those forces and realizes no reductions in the other party's forces in exchange. Unilateral reductions squander potential negotiating leverage. This is a great risk if, in fact, the United States would like to realize some level of reductions in the other party's forces. In the contemporary example of New START, the United States has engaged in unilateral reductions while it continues to have serious unmet goals with regard to the reduction of Russian nuclear forces, particularly including in Russian tactical nuclear forces and prospectively in future Russian heavy ICBMs.

27. Senator SESSIONS. Dr. Payne, the Strategic Posture Commission report states: "the United States needs a spectrum of nuclear and non-nuclear force employment options and flexibility in planning along with the traditional requirements for forces that are sufficiently lethal and certain of their result to threaten an appropriate array of targets credibly." In your opinion, does our nuclear doctrine and nuclear targeting strategy adequately address this approach today?

Dr. PAYNE. Contemporary U.S. doctrine as described publicly calls for considerable U.S. flexibility and options to support the fundamental national goals of deterrence, extended deterrence, assurance, and defense. Some elements of U.S. doctrine, such as the policy that precludes any new U.S. nuclear capabilities, limit the flexibility and options that may be important to support U.S. goals in the future. It is very difficult to discuss U.S. targeting issues openly. It is possible to observe that the current triad of bombers and missiles and the associated warheads provide flexibility and lethality that help support these fundamental national goals. However, some recent public discussion by senior officials cast troubling doubt on the future of the U.S. triad and the flexibility and options made possible by the triad. In addition, there are some U.S. targeting capabilities that may be extremely important in support of U.S. goals that either are in short supply or are unavailable. For example, as several senior military officers have emphasized publicly, available U.S. long-range prompt global strike (PGS) options are nuclear; the availability of non-nuclear PGS options could be important for U.S. national goals in numerous plausible scenarios. Similarly, some allies have openly described the U.S. nuclear force characteristics they deem important for extended nuclear deterrence and their assurance. U.S. forces with these characteristics in some cases either are aged or non-existent. In addition, the level of U.S. societal vulnerability to various types of weapons of mass destruction attack appears to be extremely high, reflecting a potential inadequacy in U.S. societal defensive assets available and as planned. Finally, the strategic offense and defense capabilities needed to support national goals in the future are bound to change over time and cannot be predicted with great precision. Therefore, ensuring that the U.S. force posture provides flexibility and has the necessary resilience to adapt to future threats must be our primary consideration. Further reductions and limitations on the U.S. force structure beyond New START could undermine that needed flexibility and resilience.

28. Senator SESSIONS. Dr. Payne, how could a policy of unilateral reductions impact our nuclear strategy and targeting doctrine?

Dr. PAYNE. Unilateral reductions could create a gap or further exacerbate the gaps in U.S. force flexibility and options that could prove necessary now or in the future to support the fundamental national goals of deterrence, assurance, extended deterrence, and defense. Unilateral reductions could also further reduce the negotiating leverage available to the United States without securing further negotiated reductions in Russian nuclear forces, including in Russian tactical nuclear weapons.

29. Senator SESSIONS. Dr. Payne, the Strategic Posture Commission report states that: "reductions in deployed forces should be made on the basis of bilateral agreement with Russia." Why is this important?

Dr. PAYNE. Bilateral agreement as the basis for reductions is important now because the United States has outstanding unmet objectives with regard to the negotiated reduction of Russian nuclear forces. Further U.S. unilateral reductions would potentially further degrade the negotiating leverage that could otherwise be available to the United States to realize these objectives.

30. Senator SESSIONS. Dr. Payne, if significant reductions are sought, do you agree all nuclear powers should be required to reach agreement and address threats like North Korea and Iran?

Dr. PAYNE. Any further reductions should be subject to extensive and serious consultation with our allies given the importance of U.S. nuclear forces to their security and their evaluations of their potential need for nuclear weapons. In addition, if negotiations for the purpose of further and very significant reductions take place, such negotiations certainly should become multilateral and effectively involve not only other nuclear powers but also key non-nuclear allies dependent on U.S. nuclear forces.

31. Senator SESSIONS. Dr. Payne, are you concerned that it has been reported that administration officials are considering further reductions independent of negotiations with Russia?

Dr. PAYNE. Yes. The United States has significant, unmet goals with regard to further reductions in Russian nuclear forces. Further U.S. unilateral reductions beyond New START would likely undermine the U.S. ability to realize those goals.

WEAPONS COMPLEX MODERNIZATION

32. Senator SESSIONS. General Kehler, in what ways will the construction of the Chemical and Metallurgy Research Replacement (CMRR) facility at Los Alamos and the Uranium Production Facility (UPF) at Y–12 impact current requirements for the size of our strategic hedge?

General KEHLER. As described in the 2010 NPR, the restoration and modernization of our current weapons complex infrastructure will provide an opportunity for the United States to shift away from retaining large numbers of nondeployed nuclear warheads as a strategic hedge. The CMRR Nuclear Facility and the UPF will provide national capabilities to support production of nuclear components critical for maintaining and managing the stockpile. With adequate funding, these facilities are projected to be fully operational in the mid-2020s timeframe.

33. Senator SESSIONS. General Kehler, without these facilities and the other elements associated with the robust plan for modernizing the nuclear weapons complex, do you believe reductions to the strategic hedge would be prudent?

General KEHLER. In the near-term, I support the retention of nondeployed warheads as a cost effective risk management approach to ensure our nuclear deterrent remains credible. Key considerations for determining the size of nondeployed hedge are confidence in the capability of our nuclear forces, stockpile, and infrastructure to address technical and geopolitical uncertainty. Hedge requirements are evaluated annually to maintain a credible nuclear deterrent and manage risk.

NEW START IMPLEMENTATION COSTS

34. Senator SESSIONS. Dr. Miller and General Kehler, the fiscal year 2012 budget provides little details on the costs associated with implementing the New START treaty. Has DOD estimated the anticipated cost? If so, what is the anticipated cost?

Dr. MILLER. DOD continues to evaluate projected costs for implementation of the New START treaty. The fiscal year 2012 President's budget request includes approximately $22.4 million for New START treaty implementation: U.S. Air Force $8.2 million, U.S. Army $0.47 million, U.S. Navy $6.3 million, the Missile Defense Agency $0.02 million, and the Defense Threat Reduction Agency $7.4 million.

Over the 10-year life of the New START treaty, our best estimate of the total cost for DOD activities associated with implementation of the treaty is currently between $880.5 million—$1,169 million. This estimate is tentative and does not include potential offsetting cost savings such as reducing operations and maintenance costs of eliminated forces. However, until final decisions are made on U.S. Air Force strategic delivery vehicles, as well as elimination methods for ICBM silos and conversion methods for the B–52 and SLBM launchers, it is not feasible to provide an accurate total cost estimate.

General KEHLER. DOD continues to identify and analyze New START implementation costs. We anticipate that future budgets will include costs for implementation.

35. Senator SESSIONS. Dr. Miller and General Kehler, does DOD intend to provide Congress the estimated cost associated with implementing the New START treaty?

Dr. MILLER. Over the life of the New START treaty (10 years), our best estimate of the total estimated cost for DOD activities associated with implementation of the New START treaty would be between $880.5 million and $1,169 million. This estimate is tentative and does not include potential offsetting cost savings such as reducing operations and maintenance costs of eliminated forces. However, until final decisions are made on U.S. Air Force strategic delivery vehicles, as well as elimination methods for ICBM silos and conversion methods for the B–52 and SLBM launchers, it is not feasible to provide an accurate total cost estimate.

General KEHLER. Yes. New START implementation costs will be reflected in future budget submissions. We anticipate the President's budgets will identify what must be started in the near-term in order to ensure successful completion by February 2018.

36. Senator SESSIONS. Dr. Miller and General Kehler, what is the current timeframe for implementing the force posture as outlined in the 1251 report that accompanied the New START treaty?

Dr. MILLER. The New START treaty provides flexibility for each party to implement its nuclear force structure changes and does not mandate a schedule for the implementation of reductions beyond the requirement that the three central limits are met within 7 years of the entry-into-force date.

The New START treaty entered into force on February 5, 2011, and the United States has until February 2018 to bring its nuclear force structure into compliance with New START treaty limits. The Office of the Secretary of Defense is working with STRATCOM, the Joint Staff, and the military departments to determine how we will implement specific provisions of the New START treaty efficiently and without undue impact on ongoing operations, what resources are required to implement these New START treaty provisions, and how we will phase and synchronize the implementation steps.

DOD is currently reviewing New START treaty implementation options in order to sequence activities in an efficient and fiscally responsible manner.

General KEHLER. As you are aware, the United States has until February 2018 to meet treaty central limits. DOD is currently reviewing New START treaty implementation options in order to sequence activities in an efficient and fiscally responsible manner.

37. Senator SESSIONS. Dr. Miller and General Kehler, when does DOD intend to identify a final force posture given the plans to date only specify a range for deployed ICBMs, i.e. up to 420 and up to 60 nuclear-capable bombers?

Dr. MILLER. DOD intends to provide a baseline force structure that meets New START treaty limits within the treaty's 7-year implementation period, as part of the fiscal year 2013 budget submission to Congress. It is important to note, however, that this baseline force structure could be adjusted in the future, for example, if the United States faced technical challenges with one triad leg and wished to shift weight toward another. The New START treaty provides flexibility for each party to implement its nuclear force structure changes and does not mandate a schedule for the implementation of reductions beyond the requirement that the three central limits are met within 7 years of the entry-into-force date.

General KEHLER. New START provides a flexible framework to meet central limits over a 7-year period. Because it is important not to make decisions today that preclude future options, DOD is reviewing New START implementation plans in order to identify critical milestones and key decision points. Examinations of alternate force structures are part of this comprehensive review.

[Whereupon, at 3:58 p.m., the subcommittee adjourned.]

○

www.ingramcontent.com/pod-product-compliance
Lightning Source LLC
Chambersburg PA
CBHW082158290526
45794CB00008B/3343